AINSLEY'S
CARIBBEAN
KITCHEN

AINSLEY'S CARIBBEAN KITCHEN

AINSLEY HARRIOTT

EBURY PRESS

10 9 8 7 6 5 4 3 2 1

Ebury Press, an imprint of Ebury Publishing
20 Vauxhall Bridge Road, London SW1V 2SA

Ebury Press is part of the Penguin Random House
group of companies whose addresses can be found
at global.penguinrandomhouse.com

Penguin
Random House
UK

First published by Ebury Press in 2019

www.penguin.co.uk

A CIP catalogue record for this book is available
from the British Library

ISBN 978 1 529 10425 7

Project Editor: Lisa Pendreigh
Art Director and Designer: Smith & Gilmour
Photographer: Dan Jones
Additional photography: Rob Partis
Recipe Developer: Alan Thatcher
Food Stylist: Bianca Nice
Prop Stylist: Tamzin Ferdinando
Illustrator: Carys Tait

Colour origination by Altaimage, London
Printed and bound by Firmengruppe APPL, aprinta druck,
Wemding, Germany

Penguin Random House is committed to a sustainable
future for our business, our readers and our planet.
This book is made from Forest Stewardship Council®
certified paper.

INTRODUCTION

Both of my parents were born in Jamaica. My father, Chester, travelled
to London in the early 1950s on a music scholarship and mum came to
study nursing. Looking into my family background a few years ago, on the
TV programme *Who Do You Think You Are*, opened my eyes to my heritage;
Jamaica's national motto – 'Out of Many One People' – really rang true. The
experience was interesting and emotional, but importantly, I came away
with a real understanding of the Jamaican, Barbadian, Saint Lucian and
Scottish connections of my family. I feel much closer to my Caribbean roots.

Food is an integral part of Caribbean life and, as such, was an important
part of my childhood. I have wonderful memories of helping my mum cook
and experiencing the patience and love that went into the food. Our house
was always busy with family, visiting relatives and friends. They were
welcomed and brought with them laughter and music. We would all sit
down to enjoy mum's delicious Caribbean spiced food and it was always
a generous and shared experience. Seeing all those happy people enjoying
the food together is probably the main reason I became a chef.

I want to show that Caribbean cooking is not just jerk chicken; there
is so much more to discover. Of course, jerk dishes are fabulously tasty and
an important part of Jamaican cuisine and culture, so I have included them
in this book along with other traditional Caribbean island dishes, such as
Ackee and Saltfish with Johnny Cakes, Rundown, Oxtail Stew and Curried
Goat with Rice 'n' Peas. I also want people to learn that Caribbean cuisine
is about cooking fresh, vibrant and tasty dishes. Home-cooked food that is
hearty, nutritious and full of flavour ... and yes, at times, a little bit spicy!

Caribbean cuisine is diverse; culturally, the islands are a melting pot
of identities, which influence the cuisine of each region. Originally, the
islands were inhabited by the Caribs and Arawaks, both Native American
tribes. The Caribs introduced chilli peppers and spice to cooking, and the
Arawaks used green sticks, called *barbacoa*, to grill their food – the origins
of the modern barbecue. Later, came colonists and the migration of Western
Europeans, Africans and Asians to the islands. Today you can taste the
history of the islands through the flavours of East India, China, Europe,
South America and Africa, all playing their part in the multicultural
society of the Caribbean.

I've travelled to the Caribbean many times, but this time – for *Ainsley's
Caribbean Kitchen* – I was lucky enough to travel to islands I'd never visited
before, and to discover and taste so many wonderful dishes. Although there

are common elements in Caribbean cooking, on my journey I discovered each island differs in its cuisine. Every island has its own specialities.

Jamaican cuisine is a fusion of many cooking techniques, flavours and spices, influenced by both the indigenous people of the island and Spanish, African, East Indian and British inhabitants. Its food is rich in flavour and full of aromatics, herbs and spices, such as allspice, Scotch bonnet chillies, thyme, ginger, nutmeg and black pepper. It is famously known for its 'jerk' – a technique used by the Maroon slaves and Arawaks to preserve the meat. Another well-known dish of the region is Ackee and Saltfish (see page 14). It's one of my personal favourites, which I've been cooking since I was young.

Trinidad and Tobago's cuisine is heavily influenced by East India, particularly its spicy sauces and unleavened breads. Popular dishes include roti (flatbreads filled with curried meats, seafood and/or vegetables together with a variety of spicy sauces) and seafood curries. Crab is a popular seafood. I made a delicious curried crab on the beach in Tobago (see page 128). You can also find African, Creole and Latin-American influences in the regional dishes, particularly in the street food scene. Chow is a popular condiment of chopped fruit seasoned with *shado beni* (coriander), garlic and chilli pepper. Try my Mustard Snapper with Mango Chilli Chow (see page 122).

Grenada is known as the 'Spice Island' and its dishes reflect its cultural diversity, with strong French, British and African influences. Traditional recipes are aromatic with local herbs and spices, such as nutmeg, cinnamon, cloves and allspice. Their specialty dish is the Oil Down – a tasty one-pot dish of vegetables, salted meat and spices. The national symbol of Grenada is the nutmeg, which is used in many local dishes. Nutmeg ice cream is a delicious treat available on the island and one you must try if you're visiting. The spice is also used in savoury dishes. Nutmeg works particularly well with pork. Try my Pork Medallions with a Rum, Cream and Nutmeg Sauce (see page 174).

Saint Lucia's cuisine is a hybrid of cookery from France, Britain and East India and, before colonisation, was influenced by the settlement of Arawaks. This can be seen in the use of spices, such as cinnamon, nutmeg, garlic, parsley and cloves. The local diet focuses mainly on fish, seafood, fresh vegetables and fruit, and you can sample barbecued seafood fresh off the boat served simply with sweet potato or spiced corn-on-the-cob. The island's national dish is green figs and saltfish, where green figs – also known as green bananas – are boiled or stewed and served with saltfish, usually as a breakfast meal. I've given this dish my own twist on page 43.

Barbadian cuisine, also called Bajan cuisine, features a mixture of influences from Portugal, Britain, Creole culture and Africa, and the island has long been associated with fine dining. Commonly used seasonings in Barbados are also popular in the UK, including parsley, garlic, marjoram, basil, thyme, cloves and paprika. When visiting Barbados, I met up with my friend Joel (*a.k.a.* Mr. Delicious!) and he kindly cooked some delicious flying fish – the national dish of the island – in his beach-side snack bus. It was just as delicious as the last time I'd had it and I hope to go back soon for more!

The beautiful haven of Dominica is known as 'Nature's Island'. Christopher Columbus first arrived in the Caribbean in 1492 and it's said that, if he returned today, Dominica would be the only island in the archipelago he would recognise. Its cuisine is influenced by French and Creole techniques, as well as dishes from Latin America. On the island you can find fresh herbs, peppers and spices that serve as the basis for Creole cuisine, while fresh-off-the-boat fish such as tuna, kingfish and flying fish are often featured on menus as the 'catch of the day'. The national dish used to be Mountain Chicken Soup, but – thankfully – as the Mountain Chicken is an endangered frog species, the national dish is now Callaloo Soup, a delicious leafy vegetable soup with spices and coconut. Fresh callaloo is difficult to find in the UK, but spinach or kale work well as substitutes. The influence of Latin America is shown in another favourite dish: Tostones (twice-fried plantain), which are a popular crispy snack (see page 50).

Antigua has long imported most of its food. The largest influence on its cuisine is from the early settlement of Arawaks and, later, Creole cookery. Two of the most popular foods grown by the early settlers are still part of the locals' diet today: maize and sweet potatoes. The national dish is Fungie and Pepperpot and I enjoyed a fantastic pepperpot dish at Beach Limerz. The locals use *fungie* (a cornmeal maize, similar to polenta) in a variety of dishes and I used it to coat another local favourite – okra – to make a tasty snack (see Spiced Cornmeal-Coated Okra with Smoked Tzatziki, page 40). If you go to Antigua, you have to try their black pineapples – oh wow! They are probably the sweetest and most delicious I have ever tried.

Caribbean food is often thought of as unhealthy – after all, there is a love of fried chicken and dishes with rich sauces. I found this misconception highlighted on my visit to the islands, when I discovered just how important local, seasonal produce is. The lush islands are full of fresh vegetables and fruits and that local produce is used in season to create great-tasting, vibrant food. By relying on fresh seasonal produce, modern Caribbean cooking is more focused on light, nutritious and fresh meals. If it's in season, there's plenty of it and the taste is sublime. Out of season, and you just have to wait!

(There are exceptions: in the posh hotels of Barbados, Jamaica, Antigua and Saint Lucia, tourists like to have foods when they want and can pay for imported produce, but, generally, everything is seasonal.)

When in season, avocados in the Caribbean are amazing – they can grow to the size of a child's head and are deliciously creamy. Mangoes and papaya (pawpaw) similarly grow to a large size and the taste is phenomenal – you feel kissed by the sun when eating them. 'Ground provisions' are an integral part of everyday cooking on the islands – the term refers to root vegetables such as yam, dasheen, cassava and sweet potatoes and can also include plantain and green bananas. They grow in abundance on the islands and are used as an alternative to rice. The use of fresh herbs and those spices so synonymous with Caribbean cooking often means there is no need to add extra salt or serve extra condiments with finished dishes. Fresh local herbs and spices are blended together to create 'seasonings' that can be stored in the fridge for weeks, creating a quick and easy way to flavour foods.

In Jamaica, some follow traditional 'ital' values (the food celebrated by those in the Rastafari movement), so they adhere to a vegan diet. Although many Jamaican and Caribbean dishes do include meat and fish, a vast number of them don't. Caribbean spices marry well with vegetables, so I've included a section dedicated to vegetarian and vegan recipes. Increasingly, vegetables are taking centre stage on peoples' plates and it was great to try so many tasty non-meat dishes on my travels around the islands.

The traditional dishes of the Caribbean still play an important part in everyday life, but are cooked with more understanding of the principles of healthy cooking. You can still enjoy an oxtail stew – just don't use a huge amount of oil. Shallow fry your fish rather than deep fry – or, if deep-frying, make sure you drain well before serving and eat in moderation. You may be surprised to know that authentic Caribbean cuisine is rarely oily. The use of marinades and rubs lends itself better to barbecuing and grilling than frying. Incorporated with traditional Caribbean food heritage, locals enjoy varied diets with lots of seasonal fruit and vegetables, which keeps a healthy balance. Taking the traditional and adding the odd modern twist is the way to go today. Instead of traditional saltfish fritters, why not add some ackee and serve with a red pepper rouille (see page 25)?

I hope you enjoy the recipes in this book and they bring you a wider understanding of Caribbean cooking. Although there are regional differences, there is a common element – a love of real food and a passion for sharing. So, get cooking and don't forget to turn up the music and feel the vibe! With the aromatic spices and exotic flavours, I promise you will be taken on a tropical journey with every mouthful. Yeah boi, dat sound good!

LIGHT
BITES

ACKEE & SALTFISH

Ackee and Saltfish is Jamaica's national dish and a must-try if visiting the country. The dish is traditionally eaten for breakfast, but quite often makes it onto the lunch menu or is served as a light bite. To make life easier, you can now buy packs of prepared saltfish fillets, with the skin and bones removed, or pre-cooked saltfish (bacalao) in tins. This version is my old favourite and is great served with Johnny Cakes (page 32).

SERVES 4

450g saltfish or
   ready-to-use salt cod
2 large eggs
2 tbsp vegetable oil
1 red pepper, de-seeded
   and roughly chopped
1 green pepper, de-seeded
   and roughly chopped
4 spring onions, chopped
1 tsp chopped fresh thyme
½ Scotch bonnet chilli
   (or similar), de-seeded
   and finely chopped
4 tomatoes, skinned,
   cut into thin wedges
1 x 450g tin ackee, drained
1 tbsp chopped flat-leaf
   parsley
freshly ground black pepper

To serve
Hot Pepper Sauce (see page
   18 or store-bought)
Johnny Cakes (page 32)

If preparing your own saltfish, place the fillets in cold water and soak overnight, changing the water a couple of times, then drain.

Bring a large saucepan of water to the boil, add the saltfish and simmer for 10–15 minutes depending on the thickness of the fish. Drain well and pat dry. While the fish is still warm, flake and remove any skin and bones (trying not to break up the flakes too much), then set aside.

Bring a separate pan of water to the boil, add the eggs and boil for 8 minutes.

Meanwhile, heat the oil in a large frying pan and add the peppers. Fry over a medium-high heat for 5 minutes until tender. Add the spring onions, thyme, chilli and tomatoes and fry for a further 3–4 minutes.

Add the saltfish and ackee and cook for 2 minutes until heated through, carefully turning over from time to time to avoid breaking the ackee.

Drain and peel the boiled eggs and cut into quarters.

To serve, spoon the hot saltfish and ackee into a large serving dish, top with the egg quarters and sprinkle with chopped parsley and some freshly ground black pepper. Enjoy with Hot Pepper Sauce for an extra kick and my Johnny Cakes.

TIP: Ackee is a delicious vegan substitute for scrambled eggs.

BUTTERFLIED CHILLI SARDINES

This is a quick and simple dish that makes a great starter or light lunch. The chilli marinade works beautifully with the rich flavour of the sardines. Butterflying sardines is not only an easy way to get rid of all of the fine bones, it also reduces the cooking time and they look lovely served on the plate with a simple salad.

SERVES 4

8 sardines, scaled, gutted, heads removed, washed and butterflied (ask your fishmonger or see the Tip below)
Watercress, Cashew and Coconut Salad (page 85), to serve

For the marinade
2 tbsp chilli paste
2 garlic cloves, finely crushed
2 tbsp rapeseed oil
zest and juice of 1 lemon
a handful of flat-leaf parsley, finely chopped
a handful of coriander, finely chopped
sea salt and freshly ground black pepper, to taste

Preheat the grill to high.

To make the marinade, mix together the chilli paste, garlic, rapeseed oil, lemon zest and juice in a medium bowl, whisking until well combined. Add the parsley and coriander, and some salt and pepper to taste, and stir through.

Dip the butterflied sardines into the marinade until they are completely covered and place them skin-side up onto a large flat baking tray. Place the tray under the hot grill for 5–6 minutes until the sardines are cooked through.

Serve immediately, with my Watercress, Cashew and Coconut Salad (page 85).

TIP: To butterfly the sardines, open out the gutted fish, skin-side up, on the work surface. Holding the tail end with one hand, firmly press along the backbone until the fish is completely flat. Turn the fish over, then gently pull away the backbone until you reach the tail end. Cut off the backbone with kitchen scissors and discard. Scrape away any remaining fine bones, or use tweezers to pick them out. Alternatively, ask your fishmonger to do all of this for you!

CHARGRILLED CITRUS-SALTED PRAWNS WITH HOT PEPPER SAUCE

My Citrus Salt goes with so many foods. Treat it as a seasoning – it's fab on chips and sweet potato wedges. Be careful when handling the Scotch bonnet chillies – use rubber gloves or lightly oil your fingers before prepping and make sure you wash your hands afterwards. For those of you who love things spicy – this hot pepper sauce really has one hell of a kick!

**SERVES 4
(AS A STARTER)**

300g large king prawns,
   peeled, de-veined,
   tails left on
2 tbsp olive oil
2 tbsp Citrus Salt (page 106)

For the Hot Pepper Sauce
1 large onion, halved
   with root intact,
   cut into 8 wedges
5 garlic cloves, whole
100g Scotch bonnet chillies,
   halved and de-seeded
a drizzle of olive oil
juice of 1 orange
a good splash of rum
a large handful of fresh
   herbs (I use tarragon,
   flat-leaf parsley and
   coriander)

Preheat a chargrill pan over a medium-high heat.

First make the hot pepper sauce. Place the onion, garlic and chillies into the hot chargrill pan or a frying pan, drizzle with a little olive oil and fry over a medium-high heat for 4–5 minutes or until nicely charred. Pop into a blender or food processor, add the orange juice, a good splash of rum and the herbs and blend until smooth. Transfer to a serving dish.

Place the prawns in a large bowl, add the oil and citrus salt and mix together. Place the prawns onto the hot chargrill and cook for 4–5 minutes or until cooked through, turning occasionally to prevent burning.

Serve the prawns with the hot pepper sauce. Any leftover sauce can be stored in an airtight container in the fridge for up to 3 days.

SPINACH, SWEET POTATO & CHICKPEA SOUP

This soup is a hearty broth that is quick and simple to make.
Once you've tried it, you'll want to make it time and time again.

SERVES 4

2 tbsp sunflower oil
1 white onion, finely diced
1 garlic clove, thinly sliced
1 tsp cumin seeds
1 sweet potato, diced
1 x 400g tin chickpeas,
    drained
2 tomatoes, roughly chopped
a pinch of chilli powder
1 tsp honey
750ml vegetable stock, hot
225g baby spinach leaves
sea salt and freshly ground
    black pepper, to taste

Heat the oil in a large saucepan over a medium heat, add the onion, garlic and cumin seeds and gently cook for 2–3 minutes without colouring. Add the sweet potato and cook for 2–3 minutes, then add the chickpeas, tomatoes, chilli powder and honey and cook for a further 1–2 minutes until the tomatoes begin to soften.

Stir in the vegetable stock, bring to the boil, then cover and simmer for 10 minutes, or until the sweet potato is tender.

Add the spinach and cook for 1 minute, stirring until the spinach wilts. Season to taste, ladle into bowls and serve.

CRAB & CHILLI CORNBREAD MUFFINS

These savoury snacks are perfect when served warm straight from the oven and extra delicious spread with butter. They're also great for lunchboxes or picnics – that is, if you can wait that long!

50g unsalted butter, melted, plus extra for greasing
150g self-raising flour
1 tbsp caster sugar
1 tsp salt
2 tsp baking powder
½ tsp ground white pepper
150g yellow cornmeal (polenta)
2 eggs, lightly beaten
300ml buttermilk
1 red chilli, de-seeded and finely chopped
a small handful each of coriander and flat-leaf parsley, finely chopped
100g white crab meat

Preheat the oven to 200°C/180°C fan/gas 6 and butter a 10-hole mini muffin tin.

Sift the flour, sugar, salt and baking powder into a large mixing bowl, add the white pepper and cornmeal and stir to combine. Make a well in the centre of the dry ingredients, pour in the eggs, buttermilk and remaining melted butter and briefly stir together until you have a smooth batter. Do not over-mix as it will make the muffins heavy. Fold in the chilli, herbs and crab meat until just combined.

Spoon the mixture into the prepared tin and bake for 10–12 minutes, or until golden and an inserted skewer comes out clean. Serve warm.

ACKEE & SALTFISH FRITTERS WITH RED PEPPER ROUILLE

This one is a corker! A great twist on a traditional Jamaican dish and perfect to enjoy with friends and a nice cold beer. Ackee is a delicate fruit with the texture of scrambled eggs, so treat it carefully when mixing the batter.

MAKES ABOUT 12 FRITTERS

450g saltfish fillets or
   ready-to-use saltfish
1 spring onion, finely chopped
1 small red pepper/sweet
   pepper, finely chopped
1 tsp finely chopped Scotch
   bonnet chilli
340g plain flour
170ml cold water
2 tsp baking powder
1 tsp paprika
1 x 280g tin ackee,
   drained and rinsed
freshly ground black pepper
vegetable oil, for shallow-frying

For the Red Pepper Rouille
2 red chillies
1 head of garlic
1 x 290g jar roasted red
   peppers, drained
   and rinsed
1 egg yolk
2 tsp smoked paprika
200ml olive oil
sea salt and freshly ground
   black pepper

If preparing your own saltfish, place the fillets in cold water and soak overnight, changing the water a couple of times, then drain.

Preheat the oven to 200°C/180°C fan/gas 6.

Bring a large saucepan of water to the boil, add the saltfish and simmer for 10–15 minutes depending on the thickness of the fish. Drain well and pat dry. While the fish is still warm, flake and remove any skin and bones (trying not to break up the flakes too much), then set aside.

Meanwhile, make the rouille. Tightly wrap the chillies and the head of garlic in foil and roast in the oven for 20–30 minutes, or until soft. Set aside to cool.

When cool enough to handle, use a small knife to peel off and discard the garlic skin and place the soft roasted garlic and chillies in a food processor, along with the roasted red peppers, egg yolk and paprika. Process until smooth. With the motor still running, very slowly pour in the oil through the feed tube of the processor until you have a smooth, thick mayonnaise. Season to taste, cover and chill until ready to serve.

In a large mixing bowl, mix together the spring onion, red pepper and chilli, then stir in the flour, cold water, baking powder and paprika until you have a batter. Add the saltfish, then gently fold in the ackee until combined. Season with a grinding of black pepper.

Heat 1cm depth of oil in a large deep heavy-based frying pan over a medium heat. Add spoonfuls of the saltfish batter mix to the pan, making sure you don't overcrowd the pan. Cook the fritters for 2–3 minutes on each side, allowing them to turn golden before flipping over. Remove with a slotted spoon to drain on kitchen paper and repeat until all the batter has been used up.

Serve the fritters with a small bowl of the red pepper chilli rouille on the side for dipping.

HOT PEPPER CRAB BEIGNET WITH LIME ANCHO AIOLI

These are deliciously light and moreish fritters – perfect for a starter or a tasty snack. Fresh crab makes all the difference, but if you can't get your hands on any then good-quality tinned crab meat is just fine.

SERVES 4

125ml whole milk
125ml water
100g unsalted butter, diced
1 tsp salt
150g plain flour
4 eggs, beaten
150g white crab meat
50g brown crab meat
1 tbsp hot pepper sauce
vegetable oil, for deep-frying

For the Lime Ancho Aioli
zest and juice of 2 limes
3 egg yolks
2 garlic cloves, crushed
1 tsp ground ancho
    chilli powder
1 tsp ground cumin
1 tsp salt
200ml vegetable oil

First, make the aioli. Place all the ingredients except the oil into a small food processor and process until well combined. With the motor still running, very slowly pour in the oil through the feed tube of the processor in a steady stream until you have a thick mayonnaise. If it is looking too thick, add a couple of drops of water. Cover and chill until ready to serve.

Place the milk, water, butter and salt into a saucepan, set over a medium heat and bring to the boil. Remove from the heat and stir in the flour with a wooden spoon or spatula until smooth. Return the pan to a low heat and cook, stirring continuously, for 2–3 minutes until the mixture begins to leave the sides of the pan. Remove from the heat and scrape the mixture into a large bowl. Using a whisk, gradually add the beaten eggs, until the mixture is smooth and shiny. Fold in the white and brown crab meat and the hot pepper sauce.

Fill a large deep heavy-based saucepan with oil to a depth of 2½cm and set over a medium–high heat. Test the oil is hot enough for deep-frying by dropping in a small piece of bread: it should sizzle and brown in 40–50 seconds.

Carefully drop no more than 6–8 dessertspoonfuls of the crab mixture into the hot oil and gently move them around with a slotted spoon to prevent them from sticking together. Fry the beignets for 2–3 minutes until golden and crispy, then remove to drain on kitchen paper. Repeat until all the mixture has been used up.

Serve with the lime ancho aioli for dipping.

JAMAICAN BEEF PATTIES

No Caribbean cookbook would be complete without a recipe for beef patties. These spicy, baked snacks are sold from street vendors' stalls, roadside shacks and canteens all over Jamaica and I ate plenty of them during filming!

MAKES 12 MEDIUM PATTIES

For the pastry

500g plain flour, plus extra for dusting
2 tbsp good-quality curry powder
1 tbsp turmeric
a large pinch of fine sea salt
1 tbsp cumin seeds, lightly toasted
250g unsalted butter, diced and chilled
50ml iced water
1 egg, beaten, for glazing

For the filling

2 tbsp olive oil
1 large onion, finely diced
3 garlic cloves, minced
1 tbsp good-quality curry powder
1 tsp ground allspice
1 Scotch bonnet chilli, finely diced
3 fresh thyme sprigs, leaves picked
1 tsp salt
1 tsp black pepper
500g minced beef
300ml beef stock

To make the pastry, sift together the flour, curry powder, turmeric and salt in a large bowl, then transfer the mixture to a food processor. Add the lightly toasted cumin seeds and butter, then pulse until you have coarse crumbs. Slowly add half the iced water, pulsing until the dough comes together – if necessary, add a little more water until the dough is formed. Scrape the dough back into the bowl and bring together into a ball. Tightly wrap in clingfilm and chill in the fridge for 25 minutes.

Preheat the oven to 200°C/180°C fan/gas 6 and line a baking tray with baking parchment.

To make the filling, heat the oil in a large heavy-based frying pan over a medium heat. Add the onion and garlic and sauté for 8–10 minutes or until soft. Stir in the curry powder, allspice, chilli, thyme, salt and pepper and continue to cook for 2–3 minutes until fragrant. Add the minced beef and cook until browned all over, breaking up the meat as you go. Add the beef stock and bring to a simmer, then reduce the heat and slowly cook, stirring occasionally, for 20–30 minutes, or until the stock has reduced and the meat is sticky and well coated. Set aside to cool.

On a lightly floured surface, use a rolling pin to roll out the chilled pastry to a thickness of 5mm, then cut the pastry into 14-cm circles. Divide the cooled beef mixture between the circles, placing the mixture on one half of each circle and making sure enough space is left around the edges for sealing. Lightly brush the edge of each pastry with beaten egg, then fold the pastry over to enclose the filling in a half-moon shape. Tightly seal the edges with the back of a spoon or the tines of a fork.

Place the patties on the lined baking tray, lightly brush with the remaining beaten egg and bake for 20–25 minutes, or until golden and crisp.

JOHNNY CAKES

The infamous Johnny Cake is one of the most loved foods of the Caribbean! There are quite a few variations on the recipe, depending on where you are; they can be sweeter or cakier or they can be flatter (like the ones I have served with the Spiced Pimento King Prawns on page 120). Johnny Cakes can be eaten for breakfast, lunch (try slicing them open and filling with your favourite cheese and meats) or dinner and can be enjoyed alongside many of the dishes in this book. They go especially well with another Caribbean classic – Ackee and Saltfish (page 14).

SERVES 4—6

225g plain flour
2 tsp baking powder
3 tsp granulated sugar
½ tsp salt
1½ tbsp butter
120ml milk
cold water, as needed
240ml vegetable oil,
    for frying

Sift the flour and baking powder into a large bowl and mix in the sugar, salt and butter with your hands. Add the milk and enough water to form a dough. Knead just until the dough is smooth and set aside to rest for 15 minutes.

On a lightly floured surface, use a rolling pin to roll out the dough to a thickness of 1½cm, then use a cookie cutter to cut the dough into circles.

Heat the oil in a large deep heavy-based frying pan over a medium heat. Test the oil is hot enough for frying by dropping in a small piece of bread: it should sizzle and brown in 40–50 seconds. Add the cakes and fry for 3–4 minutes until puffed up and golden, turning them over halfway through the cooking time. Remove with a slotted spoon to drain on kitchen paper before serving.

LOTUS & PLANTAIN CRISPS WITH PEANUT GREMOLATA & DIPPING SAUCE

Delicious, crunchy lotus root is a rather strange-looking nutritious plant, which is said to help improve the digestive system. They make amazing chips and, paired here with plantain and my spicy peanut dipping sauce, they also make a moreish snack or appetiser. Make sure you use a green plantain rather than a yellow one – it won't crisp up if it's yellow and ripe.

SERVES 4

300g lotus root/stem
1 green plantain
vegetable oil, for deep-frying
1 tsp chilli powder
sea salt and freshly ground
    black pepper
large banana leaf (optional),
    to serve

For the Peanut Gremolata
75g unsalted roasted
    peanuts, roughly chopped
zest of 2 lemons
a handful of coriander,
    roughly chopped
a handful of flat-leaf parsley,
    roughly chopped
1 garlic clove, finely chopped

For the Dipping Sauce
1 tbsp oil
2 garlic cloves, crushed
1 small onion,
    finely chopped
1 small red chilli,
    finely chopped
2 tbsp light brown sugar
4 tsp sweet soy sauce
2 tbsp crunchy peanut butter
200ml coconut milk

First, make the peanut gremolata. Combine the peanuts and lemon zest in a small bowl, stir through the chopped coriander and parsley, then add the garlic and mix until well combined. The mixture should be coarse and crunchy. Set aside.

To make the peanut dipping sauce, heat the oil in a large frying pan, add the garlic, onion and chilli and cook over a medium heat, stirring occasionally, until soft but not coloured. Add the sugar, increase the heat and cook, stirring, for about 2–3 minutes until caramelised. Reduce the heat, stir in the sweet soy sauce and peanut butter and cook for a further 5–6 minutes. Finally, add the coconut milk and cook until the sauce is the consistency of ketchup – nice and sticky, but not too thick. Set aside until ready to serve.

When you are ready to fry the crisps, peel the lotus root and plantains and slice very thinly, preferably on a mandoline. Rinse the lotus root under cold water, drain well and pat dry on kitchen paper.

Fill a large deep heavy-based saucepan or a wok with oil to a depth of 2½cm and set over a medium–high heat. Test the oil is hot enough for deep-frying by dropping in a small piece of bread: it should sizzle and brown in 40–50 seconds. Carefully add the lotus slices and deep-fry for 2–3 minutes or until crispy. Remove with a slotted spoon to drain on kitchen paper. Repeat the process with the plantain slices. Dust with chilli powder and season with salt and pepper.

To serve, lay a banana leaf (if using) on a large serving plate and place the lotus and plantain crisps on top. Sprinkle over the crunchy peanut gremolata topping and serve with the dipping sauce in a small bowl on the side.

COCONUT

Coconut, of course, famously grows all over the Caribbean. It is a symbol of the tropics and an important ingredient in Caribbean cooking. The whole 'nut' is used in many different ways, in savoury, sweet or drinks recipes, and the shell doesn't go to waste either, being often used to make jewellery, bowls or utensils. Coconut Rundown – a method of cooking in coconut milk – is a popular dish of the islands. As well as using coconut to add flavour and texture to sauces, you can also use coconut oil for frying (it's used in *Ital* cooking – see also page 46) or as a substitute ingredient in vegan cooking.

The Caribbeans were drinking coconut water long before it became a health craze. My first experience of coconut as a young child was actually in the market in Northcote Road, South London. My mum would check the weight of them and would always remind me: "the heavier the nut, the juicier it will be". Of course, we were only exposed to the coconuts with brown, hairy skin – the type that you would try to win at fun fairs. We loved the juice inside as a refreshing drink, but mostly my mum would grate the flesh into boiling water to make coconut milk for a delicious rundown.

In the Caribbean, there are a lot of green coconuts – as my late dad would say, "some as big as me head!" I can still remember my first trip to Jamaica and my uncle Harry climbing the coconut tree, chopping the coconuts down with his machete and opening them up for us kids to drink. We'd then scoop out the soft flesh to eat – divine.

ROASTED SWEET POTATO & COCONUT SOUP

Roasting really brings out the natural sweetness and flavour of vegetables. This sumptuous soup is creamy and sweet with a hint of spice.

SERVES 4

500g sweet potatoes,
   roughly diced
1 red onion, roughly chopped
1 garlic clove, roughly
   chopped
2-cm piece of fresh root
   ginger, peeled and
   roughly chopped
1 red chilli, roughly chopped
1 tbsp olive oil
2 tbsp good-quality
   curry powder
1 x 400ml tin coconut milk
400ml vegetable stock

To serve
a small handful of
   coriander, chopped
toasted coconut shards
lime wedges

Preheat the oven to 200°C/180°C fan/gas 6.

Mix together the sweet potatoes, red onion, garlic, ginger and chilli on a large baking tray or in a roasting tin. Drizzle with olive oil and sprinkle over the curry powder. Cover with foil and roast for 30 minutes, or until tender.

Transfer the roasted mixture to a blender or food processor. Pour in the coconut milk and stock and blend to a smooth and silky soup.

Pour the soup into a saucepan and gently heat through over a medium heat.

Serve, topped with chopped coriander and toasted coconut shards, with lime wedges on the side for squeezing over.

SPICED CORNMEAL-COATED OKRA WITH SMOKED TZATZIKI

These crispy, spiced okra bites are a delicious party snack, especially with – dare I say – my Rum Pu Punch (page 235)! If you haven't got any buttermilk, use fresh milk with a squeeze of lemon juice.

SERVES 6–8

½ tsp cumin seeds
½ tsp coriander seeds
½ tsp black mustard seeds
½ tsp fennel seeds
½ tsp black peppercorns
2 tsp chilli powder,
　　plus extra for dusting
1 x 200g tub tzatziki
　　(store-bought)
150g coarse cornmeal
　　(polenta)
75g cornflour
150ml buttermilk
2 garlic cloves, minced
2½-cm piece of fresh root
　　ginger, peeled and minced
175g okra, trimmed and
　　halved lengthways
vegetable oil, for deep-frying
sea salt

Place a small dry frying pan over a low heat and toast the cumin, coriander, black mustard and fennel seeds and black peppercorns until aromatic – it doesn't take long, about 30 seconds. Let cool slightly and tip into a spice grinder or mortar and pestle, add the chilli powder and a pinch of salt and grind well.

Add ½ teaspoon of the ground spices to the tub of tzatziki, stir well and set aside.

Place the remaining spice mixture into a large plastic freezer bag or bowl along with the cornmeal and cornflour.

Put the buttermilk, garlic and ginger into a large bowl and stir to combine. Add the okra and gently mix until evenly coated. Tip the buttermilk-coated okra into the spiced flour bag or bowl and shake or toss until well covered.

Fill a large deep heavy-based saucepan with vegetable oil to a depth of 2½cm and set over a medium–high heat. Test the oil is hot enough for deep-frying by dropping in a small piece of bread: it should sizzle and brown in 40–50 seconds. Carefully add the okra to the oil in batches and deep-fry for 2–3 minutes until golden and crispy. Remove with a slotted spoon to drain on kitchen paper.

Season the okra with salt and a dusting of chilli powder and serve immediately, with the smoked tzatziki for dipping.

GREEN BANANA ROSTI WITH SALTFISH GUACAMOLE

The national dish of Saint Lucia is Green Fig Salad. Oddly, green figs are not actually figs, but rather green bananas – the island's largest export. No one really knows the reason why the locals call them green figs, however here is my spin on their popular dish using the fruit with two names. Don't get your green bananas and plantains confused – although they are from the same family, they are completely different.

SERVES 4

For the Green Banana Rosti
4 green bananas, peeled
juice of 1 lemon
2 thyme sprigs,
    finely chopped
½ red Scotch bonnet
    chilli, finely chopped
3 spring onions,
    finely chopped
2 tbsp olive oil
25g butter, diced
sea salt and freshly
    ground black pepper

For the Saltfish Guacamole
1 large avocado, peeled,
    stoned and roughly
    chopped
250g saltfish, flaked
½ Scotch bonnet chilli,
    finely chopped
1 plum tomato, de-seeded
    and chopped
a small handful of
    coriander, chopped
juice of ½ lime
freshly ground black pepper

To serve
chilli oil
coriander leaves

To make the rosti, coarsely grate the green banana into a large bowl. Add the lemon juice and immediately mix together to prevent the banana oxidising and turning black. Gather the grated banana in your hands and squeeze tightly to remove any excess juice.

Put the squeezed banana into a clean bowl and add the thyme, chilli and spring onion, season with salt and pepper and stir to combine. Use your hands to divide the mixture into 8 and squeeze together into round rosti cakes – they can break up slightly, so squeeze tightly (see Tip).

Set a frying pan over a medium heat and add the oil. Carefully slide the rosti into the pan, in batches if necessary, and fry for 5–6 minutes on each side. During cooking, drop in the butter for flavour and colour. When golden on both sides, remove the rosti from the pan and drain on kitchen paper.

To make the saltfish guacamole, put the avocado into a large bowl, slightly mash with a fork then add the flaked saltfish, chilli, tomato, coriander and lime juice. Season with pepper and gently combine with a fork.

Place the rosti on serving plates and spoon the guacamole on top. Garnish with fresh coriander leaves and drizzle around a little chilli oil.

TIP: To make the rosti nice and round, use a metal food ring and press down firmly, before popping out and straight into the frying pan.

ONION OKRA BHAJI WITH HOT SAUCE MANGO CHUTNEY

Ever since the mid-1800s, with the arrival of indentured labourers, there has been a heavy Indian influence on Trinidadian cuisine. So, during my visit to the island, I re-created a popular Indian snack with a Caribbean twist. This simple-to-make sweet and spicy chutney is the perfect dip for these light and spicy bhaji.

SERVES 4–6

3 white onions, trimmed
  and finely sliced
1 red pepper, de-seeded
  and finely sliced
8–10 okra, washed, trimmed,
  de-seeded (see tip) and
  finely sliced on an angle
50–75g gram (chickpea)
  flour
2 tsp baking powder
1 tsp chilli flakes
1 tsp ground cumin
1 tsp ground allspice
a pinch each of salt
  and pepper
vegetable oil, for frying

**For the Hot Sauce
  Mango Chutney**
4 tbsp mango chutney
2 tsp Hot Pepper Sauce (see
  page 18 or store-bought)
2 spring onions, finely sliced
a small handful of coriander,
  finely chopped

First, make the chutney. Place the mango chutney in a bowl, add the hot pepper sauce and stir to combine. Add the spring onions and fresh herbs and mix together. Set aside.

Fill a large deep heavy-based saucepan with vegetable oil to a depth of 2½cm and set over a medium–high heat.

While the oil is heating, in a pestle and mortar, lightly bash the sliced onions and red pepper for 4–5 minutes, so that they release their juices, then tip into a large bowl and add the okra. Sprinkle over the gram flour so that the vegetables are lightly coated, then add the baking powder, chilli flakes, ground cumin, allspice and salt and pepper. Using your hands, massage the ingredients together so that the flour and spices combine with the juices from the vegetables. Add a splash of water, if needed, but make sure that the coating isn't too wet.

Test the oil is hot enough for deep-frying by dropping in a small piece of bread: it should sizzle and brown in 40–50 seconds. When ready, pinch small handfuls of the bhaji mixture, form loosely into spikey balls and use a slotted spoon to carefully lower them into the hot oil. Cook for 3–4 minutes, turning once or twice until crisp and golden in colour. Remove with a slotted spoon to drain on kitchen paper.

Serve with the Hot Sauce Mango Chutney.

TIP: When de-seeding the okra, use a teaspoon to easily scrape out the seeds.

ITAL

The *Ital* diet (sometimes spelled *I-tal*) has been followed in Jamaica and other parts of the Caribbean since the beginning of the Rastafarian religion in the 1920s and '30s. The word is derived from the word 'vital' (in Rastafarian culture, removing the initial letter of a word and/or replacing it with an "I" signifies unity with nature). Leonard Howell, one of the founders of the Rasta movement, was influenced by the indentured Indians and their meat-free diet and those that now follow the *Ital* diet eat only plant-based and unprocessed foods; some follow a strict vegan diet.

It's a natural way of cooking that tries to avoid additives, oil, salt (although kosher salt is sometimes used) and sugar, and the diet is said to improve health and energy. Running through the *Ital* philosophy is the Rastafarian concept of livity – that the life-force of Jah/God or life energy exists in all living things. Therefore, food should be as natural and pure as possible.

Traditionally, *Ital* food was one-pot cooking – stews of fruit or vegetables and rice, seasoned with spring onions, garlic, thyme, Scotch bonnet, allspice, nutmeg and limes – but the cuisine is now more varied as veganism and vegetarianism are becoming more popular and the stereotypes are being broken down. The food is vibrant, with delicious uses of herbs and spices with fresh produce. Caribbean spices and herbs work well with vegetables and there is an abundance of both on the islands. There are also plenty of beautiful tropical fruits to make great smoothies and healthy juices.

The *Ital* diet is all about nurturing life from the soil and growing and preparing your own food to live a better life in tune with nature – it has a philosophical and spiritual purpose. I found this when I visited Lisa and Chris at their organic sustainable farm in Jamaica, Stush in the Bush. They have a real love of the land and what it provides. They make incredible gourmet food using what they have around them – modern Jamaican cooking from the heart. They call it 'sexy vegetarianism' and, with dishes such as their golden coconut-crusted yam and pineapple croquettes, or ackee ravioli, it's easy to see why.

SPICED CORN, LENTIL & BUTTERNUT SQUASH CHOWDER

This chowder is full of the flavours of the Caribbean – the warmth from the blend of spices is delightful with the sweetness of the corn and squash.

SERVES 4 AS A MAIN
OR 6 AS A STARTER

1 tbsp olive oil
1 large white onion,
    finely diced
2 garlic cloves, grated
    or finely chopped
½ tsp cayenne pepper
200g yellow split lentils
200g butternut squash,
    roughly diced into
    2cm chunks
700ml vegetable stock
1 x 400ml tin coconut milk
1 Scotch bonnet chilli,
    halved
2 thyme sprigs
1 x 200g tin sweetcorn,
    drained
sea salt and freshly
    ground black pepper

To serve
2 tsp red chilli oil, to garnish
a small handful of flat-leaf
    parsley, roughly chopped,
    to garnish

Heat the oil in a large saucepan over a medium heat, add the onion and garlic and sweat for 7–8 minutes, until softened but not coloured. Add the cayenne pepper and cook for 1 minute, then add the split lentils, squash, stock, milk, chilli and thyme. Bring to a simmer, then reduce the heat to low and cook for 20–25 minutes, until the squash is tender and the lentils are soft, but not mushy. Add the sweetcorn, season with salt and pepper and bring the soup back to a simmer.

To serve, spoon into warm bowls and drizzle over a little chilli oil and a sprinkling of parsley.

TOSTONES WITH TOMATO & CAPER SALSA

Plantains are a starchy, unsweet type of banana and they must be cooked before eating. Tostones are twice-fried plantains and a popular snack or side dish throughout the Caribbean – especially in Dominica, where many people prefer them to chips. Once you taste these crispy Tostones with my easy-to-make, zingy salsa, it's easy to see why!

**SERVES 2–4
AS A SNACK**

vegetable oil, for deep-frying
2 green plantains, peeled
    and cut into 2½-cm
    thick slices
sea salt and freshly
    ground black pepper

**For the Tomato and
    Caper Salsa**
2–3 ripe tomatoes,
    quartered, de-seeded
    and diced
1 garlic clove, finely chopped
2 tbsp capers, finely chopped
a small handful of flat-leaf
    parsley, roughly chopped
juice of ½ lemon
1 tbsp olive oil
sea salt and freshly
    ground black pepper

To make the salsa, combine the diced tomato, garlic, capers, parsley and lemon juice in a bowl and stir together. Season with salt and pepper and drizzle over the olive oil.

Fill a large deep heavy-based saucepan with vegetable oil to a depth of 2½cm and set over a medium–high heat. Test the oil is hot enough for deep-frying by dropping in a small piece of bread: it should sizzle and brown in 40–50 seconds. Add the plantains and fry for about 3 minutes until lightly golden. Remove with a slotted spoon to drain on kitchen paper.

Spread the fried plantains over a flat surface and use the bottom of a small pan to flatten them to about 5mm thick. Return the plantains to the hot oil and fry until golden on both sides. Remove to drain well once again on kitchen paper.

Season with salt and pepper and serve immediately with the salsa.

AINSLEY'S CARIBBEAN VEGETABLE RUNDOWN

Rundown is the Jamaican name given to the technique of slow-cooking with coconut milk and spices to achieve a tasty, thick and creamy stew. Typically, the dish consists of fish (such as mackerel), coconut, tomato and spices, but in this veggie recipe I've made the vegetables the star!

SERVES 4

2 sweet potatoes, peeled and roughly diced
2 green bananas, peeled and sliced
1 dasheen, peeled and roughly diced
2 tbsp olive oil
2 spring onions, chopped, white and green parts separated
2 garlic cloves, crushed
6 large okra, trimmed and sliced
4 tomatoes, chopped
½ tsp ground allspice
1 tsp chopped fresh thyme
1 x 400ml tin coconut milk
2 tbsp Hot Pepper Sauce (see page 18 or store-bought)
sea salt and freshly ground black pepper

Place the sweet potatoes, green bananas and dasheen in a saucepan with enough water to cover and bring to the boil. Continue to boil for 15 minutes, or until everything is tender. Drain.

Heat the olive oil in a large saucepan over a medium heat, add the whites of the spring onions, garlic, okra and tomatoes and fry for 3–5 minutes. Add the boiled vegetables, allspice, thyme, coconut milk and hot pepper sauce and cook for 10–15 minutes until the sauce thickens slightly (if needed, you can add a little water or stock to loosen the sauce).

Serve, garnished with the spring onion greens.

BAKED CAULIFLOWER WITH BLACK BEANS & COCONUT

This is a fantastic vegetarian main course, with a cauliflower baked in spiced coconut milk as the star. It's a hearty dish, packed full of flavour.

SERVES 4

juice of 2 limes
1 large cauliflower, outer
    leaves and stalk removed
    and discarded
4 tbsp coconut oil
1 tbsp black mustard seeds
4-cm piece of fresh root
    ginger, peeled and
    finely chopped
2–3 garlic cloves, finely
    chopped
1 green chilli, finely chopped
2 tsp turmeric powder
1 x 400ml tin coconut milk
1 x 400g tin black beans,
    drained and rinsed
a handful of coriander,
    finely chopped
sea salt and freshly
    ground black pepper
2 tbsp toasted coconut
    flakes, to garnish

For the flatbreads
250g plain flour, plus
    extra for dusting
2 tsp baking powder
1 tsp sea salt
250g thick Greek-style
    yoghurt
vegetable oil, for greasing

Preheat the oven to 200°C/180°C fan/gas 6.

Bring a large saucepan of salted water, acidulated with the juice of 1 lime, to the boil. Add the whole cauliflower and blanch for 6 minutes. Drain and set aside.

Place an ovenproof sauté pan large enough to hold the cauliflower over a medium heat. Add the coconut oil and allow to melt, then add the black mustard seeds and cook for about 1 minute, until they begin to sizzle and become fragrant. Add the ginger, garlic, chilli and turmeric and continue to cook for 2 minutes, stirring continuously. Add the coconut milk, season with a pinch of salt and black pepper, and bring to the boil. Add the blanched cauliflower and baste with the coconut sauce. Transfer the whole pan to the oven and bake for 30–40 minutes, basting every 10–15 minutes, until the cauliflower is tender and cooked through.

Meanwhile, make the flatbreads.

In a large bowl, combine the flour, baking powder and salt, make a well in the centre and pour in the yoghurt. Bring the flour into the centre and mix together into a soft dough. Tip onto a lightly floured work surface and knead for 4–5 minutes until smooth. Place in a lightly oiled bowl, cover with clingfilm and rest for 10–15 minutes.

Portion the rested dough into walnut-sized pieces. On a lightly floured work surface, use a floured rolling pin to roll each piece of dough into a 20-cm diameter round, about 3mm thick.

Heat a dry frying pan over a medium heat. Cook each flatbread for 1–2 minutes on each side, until nicely puffed. Keep warm until ready to serve.

Remove the cauliflower pan from the oven, gently lift out the cauliflower and set aside.

Put the pan back over a medium heat, add the black beans, the remaining lime juice and coriander and stir together until thoroughly heated through.

Portion the cauliflower into wedges and place in serving bowls. Spoon over the black bean and coconut sauce, top with toasted coconut flakes and serve with the flatbreads.

CHARRED BROCCOLI WITH HOT PEPPER SAUCE & CITRUS SALT

This is a simple way to add some zing to your greens and it works perfectly with tenderstem broccoli. You can use my own Hot Pepper Sauce (page 18) or feel free to use any other store-bought hot pepper sauce you may have in the fridge.

SERVES 4

600g tenderstem broccoli
1 tbsp Hot Pepper Sauce
    (see page 18 or
    store-bought)
1 garlic clove, minced
1 tsp honey
zest and juice of 1 lemon
3 tbsp olive oil
1 tbsp Citrus Salt
    (see page 106)
1 tbsp sesame seeds,
    toasted, to garnish
sea salt

Preheat a barbecue or a chargrill pan until hot.

Bring a large saucepan of salted water to the boil, add the broccoli and blanch for 2–3 minutes. Drain, refresh under running cold water to retain the lovely green colour, then drain again and set aside.

In a large bowl, combine the hot pepper sauce, garlic, honey, lemon zest and juice and olive oil. Add a pinch of Citrus Salt and whisk together to create the dressing.

Lightly oil the broccoli, place it on the barbecue or chargrill pan and grill for 3–4 minutes, turning frequently, until charred all over. Remove to a large bowl and toss with the dressing.

To serve, place the broccoli on a large plate and spoon over any dressing left in the bowl. Sprinkle over the toasted sesame seeds and finish with a sprinkling of the remaining Citrus Salt.

CHUNKY PUMPKIN PEPPERPOT SOUP

Pepperpot Soup is a Jamaican classic. The recipe is flexible and, although it traditionally includes pig's tail or beef, I've made this a veggie delight with chunky pumpkin. Ideally a Pepperpot should contain cassareep – a thick molasses made from cassava – but as that can be difficult to get hold of, I've used pomegranate molasses. It's a hearty, warming soup with a bit of a kick!

SERVES 4

2 tbsp coconut oil
1 large white onion,
    finely chopped
1 Scotch bonnet chilli,
    finely chopped
1 garlic clove, crushed
2 tsp curry powder
a pinch of saffron
1 red pepper, chopped
    into large dice
1 yellow pepper, chopped
    into large dice
1 small pumpkin or
    butternut squash
    (approx. 1kg), cut
    into 2½-cm dice
2 large tomatoes,
    roughly chopped
750ml vegetable stock
1 x 400ml tin coconut milk
1 tbsp pomegranate
    molasses
100g spinach, washed
    and drained
a small handful of
    coriander, to garnish
sea salt and freshly
    ground black pepper

Melt the coconut oil in a large heavy-based saucepan over a medium heat, add the onion and cook for 2–3 minutes until soft but not coloured. Add the chilli and garlic, cook for 1 minute, stirring, then add the curry powder and saffron and cook for 2–3 minutes, stirring, until fragrant.

Add the peppers, pumpkin and tomatoes, pour in the stock and bring to the boil. Simmer for 15–20 minutes until the pumpkin is soft. Stir in the coconut milk, pomegranate molasses and spinach, bring back to a simmer and cook until the spinach has wilted. Season to taste with salt and pepper.

Ladle into bowls, sprinkle with small sprigs of coriander, add a grind of black pepper and serve.

PLANTAIN & CHICKPEA HOTCAKES WITH CUCUMBER & RADISH SALAD

These spicy, herby savoury hot cakes are perfectly complemented by this fresh cucumber and radish salad – delightful! If you can get hold of watermelon radishes, they make a really lovely addition to the salad as they're slightly sweeter and look striking on the plate.

SERVES 4

1 plantain, peeled and
   cut into quarters
1 x 400g tin chickpeas,
   drained and rinsed
3 spring onions, finely
   chopped
¼ Scotch bonnet chilli,
   finely chopped
1 tbsp finely grated fresh
   root ginger
1 garlic clove, finely grated
a small handful of coriander,
   roughly chopped
a small handful of mint,
   roughly chopped
3–4 tbsp olive oil
sea salt and freshly
   ground black pepper

**For the Cucumber
and Radish Salad**
1 large cucumber,
   peeled into ribbons
200g radish, finely sliced
2 spring onions, finely
   sliced on an angle
a small handful of
   coriander leaves
1 tbsp white wine vinegar
2 tbsp pomegranate
   molasses
½ tsp ground allspice
4 tbsp olive oil

Bring a large saucepan of salted water to the boil, add the plantain and boil for 15–20 minutes, or until soft. Drain.

Place the plantain, chickpeas, spring onions, chilli, ginger, garlic, coriander and mint in a food processor, and season with a pinch each of salt and pepper. Pulse the mixture together until coarse, then scrape out into a large bowl. Bring the mixture together with your hands, then divide into equal-sized patties.

Heat 3 tablespoons of the olive oil in a large frying pan over a low-medium heat. Add the patties (in batches if necessary, adding more oil as needed) and fry for 3–4 minutes, until golden and lightly crispy.

To make the salad, put the cucumber, radish, spring onions and coriander into a large bowl. In a separate bowl, mix together the white wine vinegar, molasses and ground allspice. Slowly drizzle in the olive oil, whisking continuously, until emulsified. Pour the dressing over the salad, reserving a little for serving, and toss together.

To serve, place the dressed salad on serving plates, top with the hotcakes and an extra drizzle of dressing.

COCONUT WATER, KALE & MIXED BEAN SALAD

Cooking the kale and beans in coconut water brings a lovely refreshing taste to this warm salad. If you are following a vegan diet, please make sure that your hot pepper sauce is suitable, if store-bought, or use my recipe on page 18.

**SERVES 2 AS A MAIN
OR 4 AS A SIDE**

1 tbsp olive oil
1 small onion,
    finely chopped
1 garlic clove, crushed
1 x 200g tin kidney beans,
    drained and rinsed
1 x 200g tin haricot beans,
    drained and rinsed
1 x 200g tin chickpeas,
    drained and rinsed
1 tsp Hot Pepper Sauce (see
    page 18 or store-bought)
75ml coconut water
50g kale, washed and
    roughly chopped
1 red chilli, thinly sliced
    into rings
a pinch of ground allspice
a pinch of sea salt
juice of 1 lime

Heat the olive oil in a large sauté pan over a medium heat, add the onion and garlic and cook for 3–4 minutes, until soft but not coloured. Add the kidney beans, haricot beans, chickpeas and hot pepper sauce, stir together and cook for 3–4 minutes.

Add the coconut water, kale and chilli and stir to combine. Continue to cook over a medium-high heat for 3–4 minutes, until the coconut water has almost evaporated. Stir and toss with a pinch of allspice and salt. Squeeze over the lime juice and serve immediately.

GINGER-BEER-BATTERED TOFU WITH CHILLI GINGER JAM

Ginger beer is a favourite drink in the Caribbean and I've used it here to give a spicy kick to the tofu batter. My chilli ginger jam works perfectly with these spicy, crunchy nuggets.

SERVES 4

1 x 400g block firm tofu, halved horizontally, then cut into bite-sized pieces
vegetable oil, for deep-frying

For the tofu marinade
2 tsp ground coriander
1 tsp ground turmeric
1 tsp ground allspice
2 tsp chilli flakes
1 tsp black pepper
1 tsp Jerk Salt (page 106)
juice of 2 limes

For the ginger-beer batter
225g plain flour, plus extra for dusting
2 tsp baking powder
1 tsp ground ginger
1 tsp sea salt
1 tsp black pepper
450ml ginger beer

For the Chilli Ginger Jam
1 tbsp vegetable oil
1 red onion, peeled and finely chopped
2 garlic cloves, crushed
3 red chillies, de-seeded and finely chopped
1 tbsp grated fresh root ginger
juice of 1 lime
finely grated zest and juice of 1 orange
3 tbsp clear honey
1 tbsp malt vinegar
2 tbsp tomato ketchup

To make the tofu marinade, mix together the ground coriander, turmeric, allspice, chilli flakes, black pepper and jerk salt in a large bowl. Stir through the lime juice.

Add the tofu pieces to the marinade and carefully roll to coat the pieces without breaking them up. Cover and set aside to marinate for 15–20 minutes.

Meanwhile, make the batter. In a large bowl, sift together the flour, baking powder and ground ginger. Add the salt and black pepper and gradually whisk in the ginger beer until you have a smooth batter.

To make the chilli ginger jam, heat the oil in a small saucepan over a medium heat, add the onion and garlic and fry for 2 minutes, until softened but not coloured. Add the chillies and ginger and cook for a further 2 minutes, stirring occasionally.

Squeeze in the lime juice and add the orange zest and juice, honey, vinegar and ketchup. Gently simmer for 2 minutes, to allow the flavours to combine. Remove from the heat and allow to cool slightly before serving.

Fill a large deep heavy-based saucepan with oil to a depth of 2½cm and set over a medium–high heat. Test the oil is hot enough for deep-frying by dropping in a small piece of bread: it should sizzle and brown in 40–50 seconds.

Dust each piece of marinated tofu in the flour, dip into the ginger-beer batter, making sure it is well coated, shake off any excess and carefully lower into the hot oil. Cook for 3–4 minutes until golden and crisp. Remove with a slotted spoon to drain on kitchen paper.

Serve with the chilli ginger jam.

MANGO, AVOCADO & HERB BROWN RICE SALAD

The avocados in the Caribbean are almost the size of footballs; when in season, they are available in abundance and the taste is sublime. Mixed with mango, rice and fresh herbs they make a wonderfully satisfying salad. I like to use a mandoline for the fine strips of mango.

SERVES 3–4

250g brown basmati rice
juice of 2 limes, plus grated
    zest of 1 lime
1 tsp black mustard seeds
1 tbsp olive oil
2 mangos, peeled, flesh
    removed and finely sliced
1 large ripe avocado,
    peeled, stone removed
    and finely sliced
½ red chilli, de-seeded
    and finely chopped
a handful of fresh mint,
    roughly torn
a handful of fresh basil,
    roughly torn
a small bunch of coriander,
    roughly chopped
sea salt and freshly
    ground black pepper

Cook the rice in boiling water according to the packet instructions. Drain well and allow to cool.

Whisk together the lime juice, zest, mustard seeds and olive oil in a small bowl and season with salt and black pepper.

Place the mango, avocado, chilli and fresh herbs into a large serving bowl, stir through the cooled rice and pour over the lime dressing. Lightly toss together and serve.

QUINOA & SUGAR SNAP SALAD WITH GINGER WATER DRESSING

This salad is simple, healthy and delicious. Quinoa is packed full of protein, making this a really satisfying main salad or side dish; it's also a great wheat-free alternative to other grains. You can mix up the beans and salad leaves in this dish and use your favourites instead.

SERVES 4 OR GREAT AS A BBQ SIDE DISH

100g fine beans, trimmed
250g sugar snap peas
75g fresh broad beans, podded
1 red chicory, roughly shredded
50g lamb's lettuce
1 x 250g pack pre-cooked quinoa

For the Ginger Water Dressing

100g fresh root ginger, peeled
1 tsp honey
1 tsp Dijon mustard
1 tsp sea salt
1 tsp black pepper
3 tbsp olive oil
juice of 1 lime

Bring a large pan of salted water to the boil. Once at a rapid boil, add the fine beans, sugar snap peas, then the broad beans and cook for 2–3 minutes. Drain and refresh in iced water to keep them from cooking further and to retain their colour. Drain again and set aside to cool.

Meanwhile, make the ginger water dressing. Finely mince the ginger into a bowl, collecting both the flesh and juice. Place a thin damp muslin cloth over a separate bowl and tip the minced ginger and the juice into the cloth. Bring the cloth together and squeeze tightly to express all the juice into the bowl below. This should give you 2–3 tablespoons of ginger water. Remove the cloth and discard the pulp.

To the ginger water add the honey, mustard, salt and pepper and whisk together. Slowly add the oil, continuously whisking, until emulsified and silky. Finally, add the lime juice.

Remove any skins from the broad beans, then transfer all the beans to a large serving bowl. Add the chicory, lamb's lettuce and quinoa and toss together. Drizzle over the ginger water dressing and enjoy!

SPICED CRUMBED AUBERGINE WITH BLACK BEAN & AVOCADO SALAD

Aubergine, known as eggplant in the Caribbean and the US, is great at soaking up flavours and its robust spongy flesh serves well in this recipe. My spicy crumbed aubergine is really flavoursome and, when served with the vibrant black bean salad, makes a fabulous and satisfying vegan main course.

SERVES 4

For the Spiced Crumbed Aubergine
120g panko-style
    breadcrumbs
1 garlic clove, crushed
1 tsp chilli powder
1 tsp ground allspice
½ tsp ground turmeric
a handful of mint,
    finely chopped
a handful of flat-leaf
    parsley, finely chopped
zest of 1 lemon
50ml almond milk or soy milk
75g plain flour
1 large aubergine, cut
    lengthways into 2-cm
    thick slices
olive oil, for frying
sea salt and freshly ground
    black pepper

For the Black Bean and Avocado Salad
a large handful of mint,
    finely chopped
a large handful of coriander,
    finely chopped
1 x 400g tin black beans,
    drained and rinsed
1 avocado, diced
1 small red onion,
    finely diced
2 plum tomatoes, de-seeded
    and finely diced
1 red chilli, de-seeded
    and finely diced
1 garlic clove, finely chopped
juice of 1 lime
½ tsp ground allspice
3 tbsp extra-virgin olive oil

For the spiced crumbed aubergine, combine the breadcrumbs, garlic, chilli powder, allspice, turmeric, mint, parsley and lemon zest in a large bowl and season well with salt and pepper.

Put the almond or soy milk into a separate bowl and place the flour in another bowl nearby.

Dust the aubergine slices first in the flour, then dip into the milk, and finally into the spiced breadcrumbs, ensuring they are well coated.

Heat the oil in a large non-stick frying pan over a medium-high heat. Fry the crumbed aubergine slices for 3–4 minutes, turning halfway, until golden on each side. Remove with a fish slice to drain on kitchen paper.

For the black bean and avocado salad, combine the chopped herbs in a large bowl, along with the black beans, avocado, red onion, tomatoes and chilli.

In a separate bowl, whisk together the garlic, lime juice, allspice and extra-virgin olive oil and use it to dress the salad.

To serve, place the dressed salad on serving plates and top with the aubergine slices.

GROUND PROVISIONS

Ground provisions are a staple food in the Caribbean. The term refers to a number of tuber and root vegetables such as yam, dasheen, cassava and sweet potatoes, but can also include other starchy vegetables, like plantain and green banana. They grow in abundance on the islands and are often seen as a healthier alternative to rice. Caribbean recipes will often just mention 'ground provisions' in the ingredients rather than specifying a particular vegetable, and they can be cooked and served as a side dish to stewed meat or salt fish, or added to soups and stews to soak up the flavour of the sauce. They add a unique flavour and can also thicken a dish by contributing texture.

Once seen as a 'poor man's food', ground provisions are now found on the menus of top restaurants and not just as boiled side dishes. I've used them throughout the book in many different ways – either in a bake (page 82), as a rosti (page 43) or even as part of a roast (page 162). Other than the familiar sweet potato, yam is probably the most well known of the ground provisions outside of the Caribbean. Yam is a versatile vegetable, similar to a potato; although starchy, it is also quite nutritious, with high levels of fibre, vitamins, potassium and complex carbohydrates. Usain Bolt's father hailed the yam for helping his son to win Olympic gold and, ever since, ground provisions have been seen as superfoods. Well, if they're good enough for Usain Bolt...

ROASTED KICK-UP YAMS WITH COOLING LIME YOGHURT

Yam in the Caribbean is often seen as just another 'provision' or root vegetable, but its texture is ideal for grilling and easily takes on flavours. This makes a great BBQ side dish.

SERVES 4–6 AS A STARTER OR SIDE

1–2 large yams (about 1 kg), peeled, cut into 1cm thick rounds and cut in half
2 tbsp olive oil
4 tbsp honey
1–2 tbsp Hot Pepper Sauce (see page 18 or store-bought)
150g Greek-style yoghurt
juice of 2 limes
2 spring onions, thinly sliced (both green and white parts), for garnish
sea salt and freshly ground black pepper

Preheat the oven to 200°C/180°C fan/gas 6.

Place the yam in a saucepan, cover with cold water and season with salt. Place over a high heat, bring to the boil and cook for 8–10 minutes until tender. Drain carefully and tip into a large roasting tray. Drizzle over the olive oil, 2 tablespoons of the honey and 1 tablespoon of the hot pepper sauce. Toss together and season with salt and pepper. Roast in the oven for 25–30 minutes, or until cooked-through and golden.

Meanwhile, in a small bowl, mix together the yoghurt and lime juice until well combined.

Remove the yams from the oven and, while still hot, pour over the remaining honey and toss to coat well.

Place the yams onto a serving dish and drizzle over the lime yoghurt. Sprinkle over the spring onions and, for an extra kick, add a little more hot pepper sauce. Serve and enjoy!

GRIDDLED YAMS WITH GARLIC, CHILLI & MINT DRESSING

Yams are a root vegetable and a staple food in the Caribbean. They all have tough brown skins but, depending on the variety, can have yellow, white or purple flesh. Yams can be used in the same way as you would potatoes and they have a wonderful nutty flavour. Wash your hands after peeling yams, as their starchiness can sometimes irritate your skin.

SERVES 4 AS A STARTER OR 2 AS A MAIN

1kg yam, washed, peeled and cut into 2cm-thick rounds
2 tbsp olive oil
sea salt and freshly ground black pepper
lime wedges, to serve
Barbecued Lime Breeze Prawns (see page 131), to serve (optional for non-vegans and vegetarians)

For the Garlic, Chilli and Mint Dressing

2 garlic cloves, finely chopped
½ Scotch bonnet chilli, finely chopped
4 tbsp sherry vinegar
2 tbsp honey
4 tbsp extra-virgin olive oil
a handful of fresh mint, finely shredded
sea salt and freshly ground black pepper

Bring a large saucepan of water to the boil and par-boil the yams for 10 minutes, then drain. You want them to still have a nice bite.

Meanwhile, make the dressing. In a small bowl, mix together the garlic, chilli, sherry vinegar and honey and drizzle in the oil. Add half of the mint, along with some salt and pepper to taste, and give everything a quick stir. Set aside.

Preheat the barbecue or a chargrill pan over a high heat.

Lightly brush the yams with olive oil and season with salt and pepper. Place on the barbecue grill or on the chargrill pan (don't overcrowd the pan, it's better to cook in batches). Grill the yams for 3–4 minutes on each side, then brush with some of the dressing and continue to grill, turning now and then until nicely chargrilled all over. Use tongs to transfer the yams to a serving dish.

Drizzle the dressing over the grilled yams, sprinkle over the remaining shredded mint and serve with wedges of lime. For non-vegans or vegetarians, accompany the griddled yams with my Barbecued Lime Breeze Prawns (see page 131).

SWEET POTATO & SPINACH BAKE

A delicious accompaniment for lamb or chicken, this can also be served as a veggie main with a large green salad (make sure you use a vegetarian cheese!).

SERVES 4

25g butter, plus extra
   for greasing
300ml double cream
2 garlic cloves: 1 whole
   and 1 crushed
2 thyme sprigs, plus
   1 tsp chopped leaves
nutmeg, for grating
1 onion, chopped
2 spring onions, chopped
400g (about 1 large bag)
   fresh spinach
1kg sweet potato, peeled
   and sliced into 5-mm
   thick slices
25g cheese (Cheddar or
   Parmesan or a vegetarian
   equivalent), grated
½ tsp ground allspice
sea salt and freshly ground
   black pepper, to taste

Preheat the oven to 200°C/180°C fan/gas 6 and grease a 24 x 16cm ovenproof dish with butter.

In a large saucepan over a medium heat, heat the cream, whole garlic, thyme sprigs and a good grating of nutmeg to just below boiling point. Remove from the heat and set aside to infuse.

Melt the butter in a frying pan over a medium heat, add the onion, spring onions and crushed garlic and sauté for 2 minutes, until softened but not coloured. Add the spinach, season with salt and pepper, and sauté for a further 3–4 minutes, stirring well to combine. Remove from the heat.

Layer half of the sweet potato slices over the bottom of the oven dish. Pour over the spinach mixture, then sandwich tightly with another layer of sweet potato. Strain the infused cream through a fine sieve and pour over the dish. Sprinkle with the grated cheese, chopped thyme leaves and allspice, cover with greaseproof paper and bake in the oven for about 30 minutes.

Remove the greaseproof paper and continue to bake for a further 10–15 minutes, or until the sweet potatoes are tender and the top is golden.

WATERCRESS, CASHEW & COCONUT SALAD

This is such a simple salad to make, yet it's so tasty with a lovely crunch. If you like, you can use a combination of rocket and watercress; both are readily available in salad bags and both have a wonderful peppery flavour that goes perfectly with the sweet dressing.

SERVES 4

200g fresh coconut
100g (about 1 large bag)
   watercress, washed
75g cashew nuts,
   roughly chopped
1 tbsp honey
3 tbsp sherry vinegar
3 tbsp olive oil
a pinch of salt

Coarsely grate the fresh coconut into a large bowl, add the watercress and cashews and set aside.

In a small bowl, whisk together the honey, sherry vinegar, olive oil and salt.

Drizzle the dressing over the watercress, coconut and cashews, toss together and place in a serving bowl.

CHARGRILLED WATERMELON WITH SUNSHINE SLAW & HONEY ORANGE DRESSING

Charring on a hot griddle or barbecue really brings out the natural juices and sugars of the watermelon in this delicious and colourful salad. Delightful! If you don't have any fresh coconut, you can use toasted coconut flakes.

SERVES 4

1 small watermelon

For the Sunshine Slaw
150g purple cabbage,
    thinly sliced
150g white cabbage,
    thinly sliced
100g papaya, thinly sliced
100g mango, thinly sliced
1 tart apple (e.g. Granny
    Smith), thinly sliced
a small handful of coriander,
    finely chopped
a small handful of mint,
    finely chopped
50g fresh coconut, grated

**For the Honey Orange
    Dressing**
zest and juice of 1 orange
1 tbsp Dijon mustard
2 tbsp local honey
1 tbsp salt
3 tbsp olive oil

Preheat a barbecue or a griddle pan over a medium-high heat.

First, make the dressing. In a small bowl, combine the orange zest and juice, mustard, honey and salt, then slowly whisk in the olive oil until emulsified.

Slice the watermelon into quarters vertically, then into 2½cm slices with the skin still attached. Brush the watermelon slices with the honey orange dressing and place directly onto the hot barbecue grill or into the hot griddle pan and cook for 3-4 minutes on each side, until heavily charred. Remove and set aside.

Finally, make the slaw. In a large bowl, combine the cabbages, papaya, mango, apple, coriander, mint and coconut and pour over half of the remaining dressing. Arrange the slaw on serving plates, lay the watermelon slices on top and spoon over the rest of the honey orange dressing.

WARM BULGUR WHEAT, CORN & KALE SALAD

If you've never cooked with coconut water, you're in for a lovely surprise with this delicious stir-fried salad. Instead of bulgur wheat, you could try buckwheat – it's not actually a wheat and is therefore great for those with a gluten allergy.

SERVES 4

1 tbsp sunflower oil
1 red chilli, finely chopped
1 garlic clove, finely
    chopped or grated
2 fresh corn-on-the-cobs,
    kernels removed
    (or 1 x 150g tin
    sweetcorn, drained)
100ml coconut water
1 large red pepper,
    de-seeded and sliced
1 large yellow pepper,
    de-seeded and sliced
4 spring onions, finely
    sliced on an angle
300g bulgur wheat, cooked
    according to packet
    instructions
50g kale, roughly chopped
1 tsp ground ginger
2–3 dashes of Hot Pepper
    Sauce (see page 18 or
    store-bought)
juice of 1 lime
sea salt and freshly
    ground black pepper

Heat the sunflower oil in a wok or large frying pan set over a high heat, add the chilli and garlic and cook for 1–2 minutes, stirring, until fragrant. Add the corn and coconut water and cook for 3–4 minutes, then stir through the peppers, spring onions and bulgur wheat and cook for 2 minutes. Add the kale and continue cooking until the kale just starts to wilt, then sprinkle in the ground ginger, stir through and add a few dashes of hot pepper sauce. Finish with fresh lime juice and season with salt and pepper, before giving everything a final toss.

Transfer to serving plates and kick back and enjoy – it's great served with my Carrot Ribbons with Guava, Mint and Sesame Dressing (see page 94).

GRILLED TAMARIND-GLAZED TOFU WITH SPINACH PESTO

Tofu is packed full of vitamins and protein and is brilliant for soaking up flavours. My tamarind glaze is sticky, sweet and spicy, while the pesto adds freshness. Even the meat-lovers on the team couldn't get enough of this dish when I cooked it in Trinidad! During filming I used fresh callaloo from the market, but it's difficult to get hold of here, so I've substituted it with spinach, which works perfectly well.

SERVES 4

1 x 400g block firm tofu,
    cut into 2½cm cubes
    (approx. 16 cubes)
1 tbsp olive oil

For the Tamarind Glaze
3 tbsp tamarind paste
2 tbsp soy sauce
1 tsp sriracha or chilli sauce
4 tbsp tomato ketchup
2 tbsp sugar
2 garlic cloves, minced
1 tbsp minced fresh
    root ginger

For the Spinach Pesto
25g toasted almonds
1 garlic clove,
    finely chopped
½ tbsp finely grated fresh
    root ginger
½ green Scotch bonnet
    chilli or similar
100g spinach or fresh
    callaloo leaves, washed
juice of ½ lemon
50ml extra-virgin olive oil
sea salt

First, make the glaze. In a small saucepan, combine all the ingredients for the glaze and whisk over a medium heat, until the flavours have infused and it has thickened slightly. Set aside.

To make the pesto, put the almonds, garlic, ginger and chilli into a food processor and sit the spinach or callaloo on top. Squeeze over the lemon juice and blitz for a few seconds, just until broken down. Slowly add the oil and season with salt, pulsing until the ingredients are well combined. Check the seasoning and set aside.

Preheat a chargrill pan or barbecue.

Slide the tofu cubes onto skewers, lightly drizzle with oil, then place on the hot chargrill pan or barbecue and cook until charred on each side. Brush with the glaze on all sides, then cook for another 2–3 minutes, turning to caramelise the glaze on each side.

Remove from the heat and serve warm with the pesto.

CARROT RIBBONS WITH GUAVA, MINT & SESAME DRESSING

This delicious side salad is crispy, crunchy and sweet, with a hint of the Caribbean. Add the dressing to the salad no more than five minutes before serving, so the carrot ribbons stay nice and crunchy. You can find guava jelly or jam in supermarkets in the world food section or in Caribbean stores. If you can't get hold of guava jelly, a good alternative is either apple or strawberry jelly.

SERVES 4

1kg large carrots, peeled

For the Guava, Mint and Sesame Dressing
3 tbsp guava jelly
juice of 1 small lemon
a small handful of mint, finely chopped
1 tbsp sesame seeds
1 tsp black caraway seeds (or black mustard seeds)
sea salt and freshly ground black pepper

Using a vegetable peeler or a mandoline, finely ribbon the carrots into a large bowl and set aside.

To make the dressing, whisk together the guava jelly and lemon juice until smooth. Add the mint and seeds, season with salt and pepper, and stir together.

When ready to serve, drizzle the dressing over the carrot ribbons and toss together.

FISH

BAJAN FISH FRY

Everyone loves a Friday-night fish supper, so here's my Caribbean version
– Bajan fried fish with sweet potato fries and a spicy black bean salsa.
Make sure you turn up the music and enjoy with friends and family!

SERVES 4

4 x 120g fillets flaky white fish
   (such as cod or pollock),
   skinned and de-boned
juice of 1 lime
1 small onion
½ Scotch bonnet chilli
1 garlic clove
1½ tsp Bajan Salt (page 106)
120g plain flour
100g fresh breadcrumbs
1 tsp Caribbean curry
   powder
1 tsp cayenne pepper
a large pinch of ground
   white pepper
2–3 tbsp vegetable oil,
   for frying

For the Sweet Potato Fries
2 large sweet potatoes,
   cut into fries or wedges
2 tbsp olive oil
½ tsp cayenne pepper
Bajan Salt (page 106), to taste

For the Black Bean Salsa
1 x 400g tin black beans,
   drained and rinsed
3 spring onions, finely sliced
   on the diagonal
1 garlic clove, finely chopped
½ red chilli, finely chopped
3 plum tomatoes, de-seeded
   and finely diced
1 tsp chopped fresh
   thyme leaves
a handful of coriander,
   chopped
juice of 1 lime
1 tbsp olive oil
sea salt and freshly
   ground black pepper

First, make the fries. Preheat the oven to 220°C/200°C fan/gas 7.

Place the sweet potato fries or wedges onto a baking tray, sprinkle over the oil and cayenne pepper and toss to coat. Bake in the oven for 20–25 minutes (depending on the thickness of your fries) until crispy.

Meanwhile, make the salsa. Place the black beans, onions, garlic, chilli and tomatoes into a large bowl and mix well. Add the chopped herbs, lime juice and olive oil, mix well and season to taste. Set aside until ready to serve.

While the fries are baking, rub the fish fillets all over with the lime juice, rinse and pat dry, then place in a bowl.

Put the onion, chilli, garlic and ½ teaspoon of the Bajan salt into a small food processor and blend until smooth. Scrape into the bowl with the fish and carefully mix until the fish is covered. Set aside for 10 minutes.

Meanwhile, combine the flour, breadcrumbs, curry powder, cayenne pepper, white pepper and the remaining 1 teaspoon of the Bajan salt in a shallow dish and mix well.

Wipe off any excess marinade from the fish and dip the fillets into the seasoned flour to coat on both sides.

Heat the oil in a frying pan over a medium-high heat and fry the fish for 2–3 minutes on each side, until golden brown. If you're cooking the fish in batches, you may need a little more oil. Use a fish slice to remove from the pan and briefly drain on kitchen paper.

Remove the fries from the oven and sprinkle with Bajan salt. Serve immediately, with the hot fried fish and spicy black bean salsa.

TAMARIND RAINBOW TROUT WITH GINGER & SPRING ONIONS

Tamarind is a fruit both sweet and sour in taste, which is used in a variety of ways in Caribbean cooking. Here, it adds a delicious tang to this fish dish – the aroma when you open the bag is really lovely. It also works great with snapper or salmon fillets. As you've got the oven on, why not make some simple sweet potato wedges to accompany the fish... just toss the wedges in olive oil, season with salt and pepper, and pop onto a roasting tray to roast for 20 minutes.

SERVES 2

4 garlic cloves
2 long green chillies,
    de-seeded and
    finely chopped
a small handful of coriander
    stalks, washed and
    chopped (leaves
    reserved for garnish)
a pinch of salt
2 tbsp tamarind paste
1 tbsp sugar
juice of 1 lime
2 x 350g fresh whole rainbow
    trout, gutted and cleaned
4-cm piece of fresh root
    ginger, cut into fine strips
3 spring onions, sliced
    on the diagonal
2 tbsp olive oil
1 red chilli, sliced,
    to garnish (optional)

Preheat the oven to 200°C/180°C fan/gas 6.

In a pestle and mortar, pound together the garlic, chillies, coriander stalks and salt to a smooth paste. Add the tamarind paste, sugar and lime juice and mix well.

Score both sides of the trout with three deep cuts down to the bone. Smear the paste inside the trout cavity and all over the outside so that it is well coated.

Lay out two 30cm square sheets of heavy-duty foil on the work surface and place a sheet of baking parchment on top of each. Divide the ginger strips and spring onions between each piece of parchment, piling them in the middle, and lay the marinated fish on top. Drizzle with olive oil and fold the foil and parchment loosely around the fish to enclose them in bag-shaped parcels (not too tight – you need a little air to be able to circulate). Firmly crimp the edges of the foil parcels to seal them well and place on a baking tray. Bake in the oven for 15–20 minutes or until cooked through. Check at 15 minutes, carefully opening the bag (be careful of the steam). The fish is cooked if it is opaque all the way through and easily flakes away from the bone when tested with a knife. If not, return to the oven for a further 5 minutes.

Remove from the oven and serve immediately, garnished with the fresh coriander leaves and a sprinkling of sliced chilli (if using).

MONKFISH BAKED IN BANANA LEAF

Cooking in or serving on a banana leaf not only looks fabulous, it also gives a lovely aroma to the food. Banana leaves are readily available in Asian supermarkets, but if you can't find any, simply pop the fish into foil parcels instead.

SERVES 4

4 x 220g monkfish fillets
4 large pieces banana leaf
(optional)
Quinoa and Sugar Snap
Salad (see page 73),
to serve

For the marinade
100g fresh coconut, grated
2 banana shallots,
roughly chopped
1 lemongrass stalk,
roughly chopped
3-cm piece of fresh root
ginger, roughly chopped
2-cm piece of fresh root
turmeric, finely chopped
(or 2 tsp ground turmeric)
½ Scotch bonnet chilli,
roughly chopped
2 garlic cloves,
roughly chopped
2 kaffir lime leaves
2 tbsp fish sauce
2 tbsp palm sugar

Place all the ingredients for the marinade, except the palm sugar, into a small food processor and blitz to a smooth paste. Add the palm sugar and pulse until well combined.

Place the monkfish fillets in a bowl and spoon over the marinade. Place in the fridge to marinate for about 1 hour.

Meanwhile, preheat a barbecue or the oven to 200°C/180°C fan/gas 6.

Place each monkfish fillet in the centre of a banana leaf, wrap well and secure with string or wooden skewers to create a parcel (you will need 2 skewers for each parcel). Alternatively, wrap them in foil, crimping the edges tightly.

Lay the parcels on the barbecue grill and cook for 5 minutes on each side, moving the parcels regularly to avoid flare-ups. Alternatively, place the parcels on a baking tray and bake in the oven for 12–15 minutes, until cooked through and aromatic. Check at 12 minutes. The fish is cooked if it is opaque all the way through and flakes easily. If not, return to the oven or grill for a further 5 minutes.

Serve immediately, with my Quinoa and Sugar Snap Salad (see page 73).

BARBECUE & FLAVOURED SALTS: BAJAN, JERK & CITRUS

These salts are a great way to add some zing to your barbecue or seasoning to your Caribbean dishes. They can be used to season meat, fish (see my Bajan Fish Fry, page 98) and vegetables, or can be used as a finishing salt (see my Charred Broccoli, page 59). They can be kept in an airtight container for up to one week.

MAKES 100G

For the Bajan Salt
a small handful of
    flat-leaf parsley
a small handful of
    fresh thyme leaves
a small handful of
    fresh marjoram leaves
1 Scotch bonnet chilli,
    finely chopped
2 garlic cloves,
    finely chopped
75g sea salt
1 tsp ground cloves
1 tsp ground allspice
1 tsp black pepper

In a pestle and mortar, grind the parsley, thyme, marjoram, chilli and garlic into a fine paste with 2 tablespoons of the salt. Add the ground cloves, allspice, black pepper and the remaining salt, mix well and transfer to a bowl ready for use.

For the Jerk Salt
2 garlic cloves
a small handful of
    flat-leaf parsley
a small handful of
    fresh thyme leaves
75g sea salt
3 tsp cayenne pepper
1 tsp crushed chilli flakes
1 tsp paprika
1 tsp ground allspice
½ tsp ground nutmeg
½ tsp ground cinnamon
½ tsp ground ginger

In a pestle and mortar, grind the garlic, parsley and thyme to a fine paste with 2 tablespoons of the salt. Add the cayenne pepper, chilli flakes, paprika, allspice, nutmeg, cinnamon, ginger and the remaining salt, mix well and transfer to a bowl ready for use.

For the Citrus Salt
zest of 2 limes
zest of 1 lemon
zest of 1 pink grapefruit
75g sea salt
½ tsp freshly ground nutmeg
1 tsp cayenne pepper

Place the zest of the citrus fruits into a pestle and mortar, add a small pinch of the salt and grind to a fine paste. Add the remaining salt and the spices, mix well and transfer to a bowl ready for use.

BLUE WATER CRAB CHOWDER

In the Caribbean, you are likely to come across Conch Chowder on menus, but I decided to use white crab meat instead for this dish. The waters of the Caribbean are so blue and clear and filled with an abundance of fish and shellfish – the crab is particularly sweet. Gorgeous!

SERVES 6

1 tbsp olive oil
5 spring onions, finely chopped, white and green parts separated
1 fennel bulb, finely diced
2 garlic cloves, finely chopped
½ Scotch bonnet chilli, finely diced
1 thyme sprig, leaves picked
1 tsp ground allspice
1 tbsp tomato paste
100g yam, diced
5 new potatoes, diced
1 small red pepper, de-seeded and diced
2 x 400g tins chopped tomatoes
500ml shellfish stock
500ml chicken stock
350g white crab meat
juice of 1 lime
sea salt and freshly ground black pepper

Heat the oil in a large heavy-based saucepan over a medium heat, add the whites of the spring onions and the fennel and cook for 6–7 minutes, stirring, until soft. Add the garlic, chilli and thyme and cook for a further 2–3 minutes. Stir in the allspice and tomato paste and continue to cook for 2 minutes, stirring, to cook off the rawness. Stir in the yam, potatoes and red pepper, then add the tomatoes and season with a pinch each of salt and pepper. Pour in the stocks and simmer for 10–15 minutes, until the yam and potatoes are tender.

To finish, stir through the white crab meat and spring onion greens, then squeeze in the lime juice for freshness. Ladle into warm bowls and serve immediately.

FISH & SEAFOOD

With such an expanse of beautiful, clear blue waters, it's no surprise that fish and seafood are highlights of Caribbean cuisine. Seafood is popular on all the islands; from blue water crab to spiny lobsters, you can enjoy fresh-off-the-boat seafood in most restaurants.

Conch (pronounced 'conk') is a popular local delicacy – it's a mollusc or type of sea snail found in beautiful, pink spiral shells. On menus, you'll find it stewed, fried into fritters and chopped into salads – what's more, it's said to be an aphrodisiac! Stuffed crab backs or crab curries are popular in Trinidad and Tobago (see page 128) and the crab meat I ate in the Caribbean is probably some of the sweetest I've ever tasted.

There is a huge variety of fish available around the islands, from large marlin to smaller grouper and snapper, and they are usually served simply grilled or barbecued with local herbs, or spiced up with Bajan or jerk seasoning. Flying fish (its wings are overgrown fins) are firm white fish, best served grilled or fried (the national dish of Barbados). Saltfish is a Caribbean staple and forms a base for many national dishes, such as green figs and saltfish (Saint Lucia), or saltfish and ackee and saltfish fritters (Jamaica). Saltfish is a meaty white fish (often cod) that has first been preserved by salt-curing, then dried. The most popular way of cooking it in the Caribbean is fried saltfish – although rather than being actually fried, it's instead sautéed with onions, thyme, tomatoes and Scotch bonnet chilli.

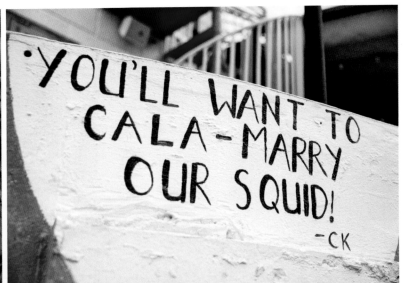

YOU'LL WANT TO CALA-MARRY OUR SQUID!

-CK

CARIBBEAN FISH CURRY WITH SPINACH & COCONUT

I love this one-pot curry; a wonderfully aromatic and vibrant fish dish with Caribbean spices and creamy coconut. You can use any fish you like, although a firm white fish such as hake or cod works best – maybe add some prawns, if you fancy. Caribbean curry powder is available from most supermarkets, but if you can't find any, use a mild Indian curry powder. Serve with Rice 'n' Peas (see page 136) or plain white rice and a sprinkling of fresh coriander.

SERVES 4

4 x 120g large white fish fillets, skinless
juice of ½ lime
2 tbsp mild Caribbean curry powder
1 tbsp vegetable oil
3-cm piece of fresh root ginger, peeled and finely grated
5 spring onions, sliced and a few slices reserved to garnish
2 garlic cloves, minced
1 Scotch bonnet chilli, finely chopped
1 red pepper, roughly chopped
1 tsp chopped thyme leaves
1 x 400g tin coconut milk
100g (about 1 small bag) baby spinach leaves
a handful of coriander leaves, chopped sea salt and freshly ground black pepper

Rub the fish fillets all over with the lime juice, 1 teaspoon of the curry powder and season with salt and pepper. Set aside.

Meanwhile, make the sauce. Heat the oil in a deep frying pan with a lid over a medium heat, add the ginger, spring onions, garlic, chilli and red pepper and cook for 5 minutes. Stir in the remaining curry powder and thyme and cook for 1 minute. Add the coconut milk and simmer, uncovered, for 8–10 minutes until the sauce has thickened.

Add the fish, pushing it down into the sauce, and cover the pan with a lid. Simmer gently for 8–10 minutes, or until the fish flakes easily. Sprinkle over the spinach and coriander leaves in the last couple of minutes of cooking. When it has softened in the steam, carefully push the leaves down into the sauce, between the fish, to avoid breaking up the fillets.

Serve in warm bowls, with rice and a sprinkling of the reserved spring onion slices.

JERK SNAPPER WITH OKRA SALSA

Okra is widely used in Caribbean cooking and is a tasty, nutritious little vegetable that adds a nice bite to my salsa. Look for firm, bright green pods and avoid any that are limp with brown marks – these are not so fresh. This lightly-spiced fish dish can be prepared in the oven or on a barbecue and it goes well with fresh crusty bread, to soak up all the juices.

SERVES 2

2 x 400g whole snapper,
    tilapia or similar, scaled,
    gutted and cleaned
juice of 1 lime
1–2 tbsp Jerk Salt (page 106)
2 tsp butter, plus extra
    for greasing
fresh bread, to serve

For the Okra Salsa
175g okra, trimmed,
    halved and de-seeded
zest and juice of 1 lemon
2 garlic cloves, minced
a handful of flat-leaf
    parsley, chopped
sea salt and freshly ground
    black pepper, to taste

Rub the fish all over, inside and out, with lime juice and score three deep slits across the body of each. Mix the jerk salt with the butter and rub the seasoned butter all over the fish, including inside the cavities. Leave to marinate for 1 hour.

Meanwhile, preheat a barbecue or the oven to 200°C/180°C fan/gas 6 and butter two large sheets of foil or baking parchment.

Place each fish on a piece of greased foil or parchment and wrap loosely but securely, so that the juices or steam can't escape. Place on a baking sheet and bake in the oven for 12–15 minutes (depending on the size of the fish) and leave to rest for a few minutes before serving. Alternatively, cook directly on the barbecue grill, turning it halfway through. Make sure you don't overcook – the fish is done when it is opaque all the way through and easily flakes away from the bone.

Finely chop the okra and put into a bowl. Add the lemon zest and juice, minced garlic and parsley, season with salt and pepper and mix well, then set aside.

Carefully open the fish parcels and serve with the cooking juices, okra salsa and some fresh bread.

MACKEREL ESCOVITCH

Escovitch Fish is a traditional Caribbean recipe of fried or grilled fish
marinated in a spiced pickling liquor; it's tart, spicy and a little sweet.
The dish can be eaten hot or cold and is best served with bread for
mopping up the liquor.

SERVES 4

4 x 100–125g large mackerel
   fillets, pin-boned and cut
   in half on an angle
3 tbsp Bajan Salt (page 106)
1 carrot, peeled and finely
   shredded (ideally on
   a mandoline)
1 large shallot, peeled and
   finely shredded (ideally
   on a mandoline)
1 red pepper, finely shredded
   (ideally on a mandoline)
½ cucumber, halved,
   de-seeded and finely
   shredded (ideally on
   a mandoline)
watercress or rocket leaves,
   to serve

For the pickling liquor
300ml white wine vinegar
200ml water
2 bay leaves
1 tsp salt
1 tbsp sugar
6 white peppercorns
5 pimento berries
1 dried red chilli

Lay the mackerel fillets in a deep roasting tray, skin-side down,
and check again for small pin bones. Lightly season with the
Bajun salt, making sure it is well covered, then cover with
clingfilm and place in the fridge.

Meanwhile, in a non-metallic saucepan, combine the pickling
liquor ingredients and bring to the boil. Add the shredded
vegetables and stir to combine. Remove from the heat and
set aside to cool a little.

Remove the mackerel from the fridge and turn the fillets
skin-side up. Pour over the warm pickled vegetables, making
sure the mackerel is well submerged. Cover tightly with
clingfilm and chill for a further 1–2 hours.

Preheat the grill to hot.

Remove the mackerel fillets from the pickling liquor and place
under the grill, skin-side up, for 3–4 minutes or until crispy.

Meanwhile, drain the pickled vegetables, reserving the liquor.

Evenly spread the pickled vegetables over a large serving
plate, then lay the Bajan mackerel on top. Spoon a little of the
pickling liquor around the plate and serve with watercress
or rocket salad.

PIMENTO PRAWNS WITH APPLE GINGER SLAW ON JOHNNY CAKES

These lightly griddled Johnny Cakes make a perfect base for my fresh, zingy slaw and spicy king prawns. Yum!

SERVES 4

20 king prawns
1 tsp ground pimento
a pinch of sea salt
1 tsp black pepper, plus an
    extra pinch for seasoning
1 tsp cayenne pepper, plus an
    extra pinch for seasoning
50ml vegetable oil
2 garlic cloves, crushed
1 tsp finely diced root ginger
1 red onion, finely diced
1 red pepper, finely diced
2 spring onions, finely sliced
zest and juice of 1 orange
a splash of dark rum
1 tsp brown sugar
4 tomatoes, halved and
    de-seeded, then diced
1 tsp chopped fresh
    coriander, to garnish

For the Johnny Cakes
200g self-raising flour
1 tsp sugar
1 tsp salt
50g butter
4 tbsp coconut oil

For the Apple Ginger Slaw
juice of 2 limes
5-cm piece of root ginger,
    peeled and finely grated
2 tsp light muscovado sugar
2 tbsp light soy sauce
½ Chinese cabbage, sliced
1 large carrot, peeled and
    cut into julienne
2 red eating apples, cored
    and cut into julienne
4 spring onions, finely sliced
a handful of coriander leaves

First, make the dough for the Johnny cakes. Sift the flour, sugar and salt into a bowl, then rub in the butter with your fingertips. Make a well in the centre and gradually mix in 125ml water until you have a stiff dough. Turn out onto a lightly floured work surface and knead the dough until smooth and elastic, then place in a clean bowl, cover with clingfilm and chill for 10–15 minutes.

Lightly dust the prawns with the ground pimento, a pinch each of salt and pepper and a pinch of cayenne pepper and set aside for 10 minutes, to allow the flavours to be absorbed.

Meanwhile, make the slaw. Mix together the lime juice, ginger, sugar and soy sauce in a large bowl until the sugar has dissolved. Add the cabbage, carrot, apple, spring onions and coriander leaves and toss together. Set aside.

Preheat a griddle pan over a medium heat.

Remove the dough from the fridge and cut into 4 equal pieces. On a lightly floured surface, use a rolling pin to roll the dough into 6-cm diameter circles. Brush each with coconut oil and place on the hot griddle pan. Cook for 2–3 minutes on each side, until each cake is lightly marked and cooked through. Keep warm while you cook the prawns.

Heat a large frying pan over a medium heat, add 1 tablespoon of the oil, then add the garlic, ginger, red onion, red pepper, spring onions and 1 teaspoon each of black pepper and cayenne pepper, and cook, stirring, for 2 minutes. Stir in the orange zest and juice, dark rum, brown sugar and the tomatoes and cook for a further 5 minutes. Add the seasoned prawns and cook for a further 5–7 minutes, until the prawns are cooked through.

To serve, place the Johnny Cakes on serving plates, top with the slaw and then the king prawns and garnish with chopped fresh coriander.

MUSTARD SNAPPER WITH MANGO CHILLI CHOW

Mango chow is a fruity, spicy Caribbean version of coleslaw and it's the perfect accompaniment to my mustard snapper. Triple-dipping the fish creates a terrific crispy coating and other types of fish, such as bass, work equally well.

SERVES 4

100g plain flour
1 tbsp black mustard seeds
1 tsp chilli powder
2 tbsp finely chopped
    fresh coriander
4 boneless and skinless
    snapper fillets
    (approx. 120g each)
3–4 tbsp water
4 tbsp olive oil
sea salt and freshly
    ground black pepper

For the mint dressing
a large handful of mint,
    finely chopped
1 x 150g tub natural yoghurt
juice of 1 lemon
a pinch of chilli powder
sea salt and freshly ground
    black pepper

For the Mango Chilli Chow
2 red onions, finely sliced
1–2 green chillies, de-seeded
    and thinly sliced
1 mild red chilli,
    thinly sliced
2-cm piece of fresh root
    ginger, peeled and finely
    chopped or grated
1 large firm green mango,
    peeled and finely sliced
    into strips
a large handful of
    coriander leaves
sea salt and freshly
    ground black pepper

For the mint dressing, combine the mint, yoghurt and lemon juice in a bowl and mix well. Stir in the chilli powder, season to taste and set aside.

To make the mango chilli chow, place the red onions in a bowl with the chillies, ginger, mango and coriander. Mix together, season with a pinch each of salt and pepper and set aside.

Mix the flour with the black mustard seeds, chilli powder and chopped coriander on a shallow plate and season with salt and a little black pepper. Dip the fish fillets into the flour, turning them over to cover both sides. Remove and, using your fingers, splash with water on both sides. Repeat this process 2–3 times.

Heat the oil in a large frying pan over a medium heat. Place the snapper fillets into the pan and cook for 3–4 minutes on each side, until crisp and golden. Remove to drain on kitchen paper.

Place the crispy mustard snapper on serving plates, top with the mango chow and serve immediately with the mint dressing.

COCONUT TEMPURA LOBSTER WITH RUM PINEAPPLE SALSA & PIÑA COLADA SAUCE

This dish looks great on the plate and is a joy to eat. Sweet, savoury, spicy and fruity, all with a little kick of rum – what's not to like? The sweet sauce and spicy salsa are a perfect match for the delicate and lightly crisp lobster tails. Tempura batter should be cold – remember, the colder the batter, the crispier the tempura. If it's too warm, you can always add a handful of ice cubes to cool it down.

SERVES 4

sunflower oil, for deep-frying
125g plain flour
75g cornflour
1 egg, beaten
200ml soda water, chilled
4 x 175g lobster tails, cut
   in half lengthways and
   meat removed
200g desiccated coconut

**For the Rum Pineapple
Salsa**
1 tbsp olive oil
1 red onion, finely chopped
1 red pepper, finely chopped
½ red Scotch bonnet chilli,
   de-seeded and finely
   chopped
½ small pineapple, peeled
   and finely chopped
100ml golden rum
3 Thai basil sprigs, roughly
   shredded (or leave whole
   if leaves are small)

For the Piña Colada Sauce
150ml coconut cream
150ml pineapple juice
1 small red chilli, halved
1 garlic clove, crushed
2 tbsp double cream
   (optional)

First, make the salsa. Heat the oil in a large sauté pan over a high heat, add the red onion and sauté for 2–3 minutes, stirring continuously. Add the red pepper and chilli and continue to cook for 1–2 minutes. Add the pineapple, making sure it doesn't catch on the bottom, and cook for a further 3–4 minutes, continuously stirring and tossing (if you're brave enough), then remove from the heat. Deglaze the pan with the golden rum and flambé to burn off the alcohol. Place the pan back on the heat and reduce until slightly sticky, then remove from the heat and set aside.

To make the piña colada sauce, combine all of the ingredients in a small pan, bring to a simmer and continue to cook until slightly reduced and thickened. Remove from the heat and set aside until ready to serve.

Fill a large deep heavy-based saucepan with sunflower oil to a depth of 4cm and set over a medium–high heat. Test the oil is hot enough for deep-frying by dropping in a small piece of bread: it should sizzle and brown in 40–50 seconds.

To make the tempura batter, mix together the flour, cornflour, egg and chilled soda water in a large bowl. Place the lobster tails into the batter, making sure they are well coated, shake off any excess batter, then roll the lobster tails in the desiccated coconut.

Carefully lower the lobster tails into the hot oil and fry for 3–4 minutes or until golden and crispy. Use a slotted spoon to remove to drain on kitchen paper.

To serve, spoon the pineapple salsa down the length of a long plate. Stir the Thai basil into the piña colada sauce, then drizzle the sauce over and around the pineapple and place the crispy lobster tails on top. For a more casual supper with friends, serve the lobster tails in a serving dish in the centre of the table with the salsa and the pina colada on the side for dipping – tuck in and enjoy!

TOBAGO CURRIED CRAB WITH CLAP-HAND ROTI

Tobago has one of the most varied cuisines of the Caribbean, featuring influences from Africa, China, India, Latin-America and the Middle East. Curried Crab is a classic dish of the island and is definitely a must-try if you are lucky enough to visit. Traditionally served with dumplings, I'm serving my version with clap-hand roti to mop up the tasty sauce.

SERVES 4

2 tbsp olive oil
3 spring onions,
    finely chopped
3-cm piece of fresh ginger
    root, grated or minced
3-cm piece of fresh turmeric,
    grated or minced (or 1 tsp
    ground turmeric)
1 tsp cumin seeds
2 garlic cloves, grated
    or minced
2 tbsp curry powder,
    mixed with 3 tbsp water
a small handful of coriander
    or chadon beni, roughly
    chopped, plus extra
    to garnish
500ml fish stock
1 x 400ml tin coconut milk
1kg cooked crab claws,
    divided at the knuckle
    and lightly cracked
1 small Scotch bonnet chilli
juice of 1 lime
1 tbsp white sugar
sea salt and freshly ground
    black pepper, to taste

For the Clap-Hand Roti
225g plain flour, plus
    extra for dusting
1 tsp baking powder
1 tsp salt
40g chilled butter
5 tbsp water
melted butter or light
    olive oil, for brushing

Heat the oil in a large saucepan over a medium heat, add the onions, ginger and turmeric and fry for 3–4 minutes, stirring continuously, until softened and aromatic. Add the cumin seeds and garlic and cook for 1 minute, then gently stir in the curry paste and coriander, followed by the fish stock and coconut milk. Cover with a lid and bring to the boil, then reduce the heat and simmer for 25–30 minutes until the sauce is slightly reduced.

Meanwhile, make the clap-hand roti. Sift the flour, baking powder and salt into a bowl or food processor, add the butter and blend until the mixture looks like fine breadcrumbs. Transfer to a bowl and stir in the water to make a stiff, but pliable dough. Cover and leave in a warm place for 30 minutes.

Knead the dough on a lightly floured surface until smooth. Divide the dough into 8 equal-sized balls and, using flattened hands or a rolling pin, roll out to 10cm diameter rounds, about 5mm thick. Brush each with plenty of melted butter or oil. Fold them in half, then into quarters, then roll back into balls. Roll out again to 10cm rounds.

Heat a dry, heavy-based frying pan or flat griddle over a medium heat. Brush each roti with a little more butter or oil and add to the pan and cook for 3–4 minutes, turning frequently and brushing with melted butter or oil each time. Remove from the pan, allow to cool slightly, then place in the palm of your hand and quickly clap your hands together 4–6 times to slightly separate the leaves (if they are too warm, do the clapping in a tea towel). Wrap in foil to keep warm while you cook the rest.

Remove the lid of the saucepan and stir in the crab and the Scotch bonnet chilli. Simmer for a further 10–15 minutes, until the crab is thoroughly heated through. To finish, squeeze in the lime juice and add just enough sugar to balance the flavours. Taste for seasoning, remove the whole chilli and serve scattered with the chopped coriander, with the clap-hand roti on the side.

BARBECUED LIME BREEZE PRAWNS

I was lucky enough to make this dish on the stunning beach of the Jamaica Inn – what an outdoor kitchen! These zesty, tasty prawns are perfect for a summer barbecue or put them under the grill for a quick weekday meal.

SERVES 4 AS A STARTER OR 2 AS A MAIN

4 limes: zest and juice of 2; 2 cut into wedges
2 tsp palm sugar
2 garlic cloves, finely chopped
120ml coconut milk
6 tbsp dark soy sauce
450g large king prawns, peeled, leaving the tails on
sea salt and freshly ground black pepper
Griddled Yams with Garlic, Chilli and Mint Dressing (see page 81), to serve (optional)

Preheat the barbecue or grill to medium heat.

If using wooden skewers, soak them in a bowl of water for 10 minutes.

Combine the lime zest and juice and palm sugar in a bowl and give it a quick stir to break down any little nuggets of sugar. Add the garlic, coconut milk and soy sauce, season with salt and pepper and stir to combine. Add the prawns, mix together and set aside to marinate for 10–15 minutes.

Thread 3–4 prawns onto each skewer with a lime wedge in between each one.

Barbecue or grill the skewers over a medium heat for 2–3 minutes, turning continuously.

Serve with my Griddled Yams with Garlic, Chilli and Mint Dressing (see page 81).

COFFEE CHILLI BEEF WRAPS

In the Caribbean, you are far more likely to be eating a bammy than a tortilla. The traditional bammies – a flatbread made from cassava – do resemble tortillas and so, when sampling one on the islands, I thought they'd go so well with my Coffee Chilli Beef. Tortillas are easier to find over here, but – by all means – if you can find and want to use bammies, please do!

SERVES 4

For the Coffee Chilli Beef
1 tbsp vegetable oil
1 onion, finely chopped
2 garlic cloves,
    finely chopped
2 red chillies, de-seeded
    and finely chopped
500g minced beef
1 tsp Chinese five-spice
    powder
1 x 400g tin kidney
    beans, drained
1 x 400g tin chopped
    tomatoes
150ml freshly made
    strong black coffee
sea salt and freshly
    ground black pepper

To serve
4 large or 8 small tortilla
    wraps (or bammies,
    if you can find them)
shredded lettuce
soured cream
paprika, for sprinkling

Heat the oil in a large saucepan over a medium heat, add the onion, garlic and chillies and cook, stirring, for 3–4 minutes until beginning to soften. Add the minced beef and Chinese five-spice and cook for a further 3–4 minutes, stirring, until the meat begins to brown.

Add the kidney beans, tomatoes and coffee, bring to the boil and simmer for 20 minutes until the mixture is thick and fairly dark in colour. Season to taste.

To serve, sprinkle shredded lettuce over the wraps, then divide the chilli beef mixture between them. Top with a spoonful of soured cream and a sprinkling of paprika, then fold up the wraps to enclose the filling. A glass of chilled beer (maybe a Red Stripe!) is always a winner with these wraps.

CURRIED GOAT WITH RICE 'N' PEAS

Oh, I love this dish! My mum would cook Rice 'n' Peas most Sundays, but Curried Goat was usually saved for special occasions. It's a traditional Jamaican dish with a rich blend of spices and it really packs a punch! You can use beef or lamb if you can't find goat.

SERVES 4

1kg goat shoulder
    (or mutton), diced
2 tbsp good-quality mild
    curry powder
1 tbsp ground pimento seeds
2 tsp garam masala
¼ tsp ground cloves
½ tsp ground turmeric
½ tsp ground cinnamon
3 thyme sprigs
3 tbsp olive oil
1 large white onion,
    finely diced
3 garlic cloves, crushed
50g fresh root ginger,
    finely grated
2 Scotch bonnet chillies,
    finely chopped
1 x 400g tin chopped
    tomatoes
1 litre beef stock
a pinch each of sea salt
    and black pepper
a handful of fresh
    coriander, chopped

For the Rice 'n' Peas
1 tbsp sunflower oil
25g butter
1 onion, finely diced
2 garlic cloves,
    finely chopped
450g long-grain rice
2 thyme sprigs
1 x 400g tin red kidney beans
125g creamed coconut,
    coarsely grated
1 litre hot water
1 Scotch bonnet chilli, whole
a pinch of sea salt

Marinate the meat the night before. Toss together the diced goat, curry powder, spices and thyme sprigs in a large bowl, ensuring the meat is well coated with the spices. Cover and chill in the fridge overnight.

Preheat the oven to 180°C/160°C fan/gas 4.

Heat the oil in a large heavy-based ovenproof saucepan with a lid over a medium heat. Add the marinated goat and brown all over (this can be done in batches, if needed). Make sure the pan isn't too hot or the spices will burn. Once browned, remove from the pan and set aside.

Add the onion to the same pan and cook for 5–6 minutes until softened, then add the garlic, ginger and chillies and cook for a further 2–3 minutes. Return the meat to the pan, add the chopped tomatoes and beef stock, stir well and bring to a simmer. Season with salt and pepper.

Cover the pan with a lid and transfer to the oven to cook for 2 hours or until the goat is tender.

Meanwhile, make the rice 'n' peas. Place a large heavy-based saucepan over a medium heat and add the oil and butter. Once the butter starts to bubble, add the onion and garlic and cook for 2 minutes, until soft but not coloured. Stir in the rice and thyme until everything is well coated in the oil. Pour in the kidney beans (including the liquid from the tin), add the grated creamed coconut and cook, stirring, until the coconut has dissolved and the mixture has become creamy. Pour in the water, drop in the whole chilli and stir in the salt. Bring to the boil, cover with a lid, then reduce the heat and simmer for 25–30 minutes until cooked through.

Remove the pan from the heat and let rest for 5 minutes. Remove and discard the thyme and chilli before serving.

Remove the curried goat from the oven, stir in the chopped coriander and serve with the rice 'n' peas.

JERK

Jerk is one of the most well-known dishes to have travelled out of the Caribbean in recent times. Originally, it was a method of preserving meat, said to date back to the 1700s and the Maroon slaves who escaped capture from the British army. They developed a method of spicing the meat and wrapping it in banana leaves until it was ready to be cooked over hot coals. The term 'jerk' is said to come both from the action of 'jerking', which refers to the poking of holes in the meat to allow the flavours to fully infuse, and the word '*charqui*', which is a Spanish term for dried meat. Traditionally cooked in firepits in the ground, today jerk is often cooked in 'jerk pits' – steel drums cut in half and turned into grills.

From street food to upmarket restaurant fare, jerk is an important part of island food culture. Everywhere you go in Jamaica, everyone has their own version of jerk. In fact, it seems to be the same all over the Caribbean, where you can just about jerk anything. The most popular meat to jerk is chicken, followed by pork, but you can also jerk vegetables, fish, tofu and even fruit.

Most people like to keep their jerk seasoning recipe a secret – I tried very hard to get the secret ingredients from the chef at Scotchies in Jamaica! Two ingredients that an authentic jerk seasoning *must* contain are allspice and Scotch bonnet chilli peppers. Other flavourings that are often added include thyme, cloves, cinnamon, spring onions, garlic, ginger, sugar and sometimes a good dash of rum. You can jerk an ingredient dry with a rub, or jerk it wet with a marinade. Once the meat, fish or vegetables have been marinated and cooked slowly over smoking pimento wood, the end result is a wonderful spicy, piquant delight that's exploding with flavour. Make it fresh or buy it commercially, but – more importantly – just get jerking...

HIS ESTABLISHMENT HAS 3 MICHELIN TIRES

BUTTERFLIED LAMB IN JERK BUTTER WITH PUMPKIN CHUTNEY

This is a fantastic weekend barbecue recipe. I've included a recipe for Jerk Butter, but to make life simpler you can add a tablespoon of store-bought jerk seasoning to some butter and brush over the lamb, if wished.

SERVES 4—6

8 rosemary sprigs,
   finely chopped
3 large garlic cloves
zest of 2 lemons
a pinch of sea salt
1 x 2kg leg of lamb,
   butterflied (see tip)
3 tbsp olive oil

For the Pumpkin Chutney
2 tbsp olive oil
1 large white onion,
   peeled and finely diced
1 Scotch bonnet chilli,
   split in half
25g fresh ginger,
   finely grated
2 garlic cloves, finely grated
1 tbsp black mustard seeds
300ml cider vinegar
200g caster sugar
500g pumpkin, peeled
   and diced
1 red pepper, de-seeded
   and finely diced
600ml water
a pinch of sea salt

For the Jerk Butter
150g unsalted butter
50ml olive oil
½ tbsp ground allspice
½ tsp ground ginger
½ tsp cayenne pepper
½ tsp ground black pepper
½ tsp ground cinnamon
2 garlic cloves,
   finely chopped
½ Scotch bonnet chilli,
   finely chopped
zest and juice of 1 lime

In a pestle and mortar, pound together the rosemary, garlic, lemon zest and salt into a paste. Rub the paste all over the lamb, making sure it's thoroughly worked in. Cover with clingfilm and marinate for at least 2 hours or ideally overnight.

Meanwhile, make the chutney. Heat the oil in a heavy-based saucepan, add the onions and cook for 5–6 minutes, stirring, until soft. Add the chilli, ginger, garlic and mustard seeds and cook for 2–3 minutes until fragrant. Add the vinegar and sugar and bring to a simmer, then add the pumpkin, red pepper and water. Bring back to a simmer, season with salt and gently cook for 30–35 minutes, until the pumpkin is tender and the liquid has reduced. Set aside until ready to serve.

To make the jerk butter, heat the butter and oil together in a small saucepan until the butter has melted. Add all the spices, garlic and Scotch bonnet chilli and gently cook for 2–3 minutes until fragrant. Remove from the heat and stir in the lime zest and juice.

Preheat a barbecue or oven to 200°C/180°C fan/gas 6.

Remove the marinated lamb from the fridge and lightly oil. Place the lamb on the hottest part of the barbecue grill and seal on both sides, keeping the lamb moving so that the meat caramelises all over but doesn't burn. Move the lamb to a cooler part of the barbecue and brush with the jerk butter. Cook the lamb for 40–45 minutes, flipping it every 10 minutes and brushing with more jerk butter (this will give you medium-rare lamb). Remove from the heat and let rest for 15 minutes before carving. Alternatively, roast the lamb in the hot oven for 30–40 minutes for medium-rare, basting frequently.

To serve, carve the lamb and serve with the pumpkin chutney.

TIP: To butterfly the leg of lamb, place the joint, meatier-side down, on a large chopping board. With your fingers, find where the long bone running down the length of the leg feels close to the surface. Using a sharp knife, split open the meat vertically along the bone and carefully peel it back from either side. At the furthest end is a group of smaller bones – continue to cut the meat away from these bones to completely open the leg up and lift the bones out. Cut away any excess fat and sinew. Alternatively, ask your friendly butcher to do it for you!

AINSLEY'S ULTIMATE JERK CHICKEN

'Jerking' is all about maximising flavour. The great thing about jerk cooking is that you can use either a dry rub or a wet marinade, which means that you can use the wonderful flavours in such a variety of dishes, from meat or fish, to vegetables or grains. Traditionally, the mix will include allspice and Scotch bonnet chillies, but the spices can be adapted to taste. Here's my ultimate jerk marinade with spatchcocked chicken. If you prefer, you can use four chicken breasts with the skin on and cook on the barbecue for 15–20 minutes.

SERVES 4

1 x 1.5kg chicken, backbone removed and spatchcocked (ask your butcher to do this)
mixed salad or coleslaw, to serve

For the Jerk Marinade
225g onions, peeled and quartered
2 small Scotch bonnet chillies, halved and de-seeded
50g fresh root ginger, peeled and roughly chopped
3-cm piece of fresh turmeric root, peeled and roughly chopped (or use 1 tbsp ground turmeric)
½ tsp ground allspice
15g fresh thyme leaves
120ml white wine vinegar
120ml dark soy sauce
sea salt and freshly ground black pepper

First, make the marinade. Place all the ingredients, except the seasoning, into a food processor and pulse until smooth. Season with a little salt and a generous grinding of black pepper.

Cut slashes into the smooth side of the spatchcocked chicken so that the marinade can penetrate the flesh and place the chicken in a shallow dish. Pour over the marinade and rub well into the meat. Cover and chill for at least 2–3 hours, or preferably overnight, turning every now and then.

Preheat a barbecue with a lid and take the chicken out of the fridge to come up to room temperature.

Cook the chicken on the hot barbecue with the lid down for 40–50 minutes, turning occasionally and basting with any leftover marinade, until the juices run clear when the thickest part of the thigh is pierced with a thin metal skewer.

Remove the chicken from the heat and rest for a few minutes, then serve with a simple mixed salad or a traditional crunchy coleslaw.

DUTCHIE POT PEANUT BUTTER CHICKEN STEW

This is a hearty, easy one-pot meal, full of comforting flavours and spice. It's great to use a traditional Dutchie pot, or Dutch oven, if you have one – I always use my mum's old one. If not, a casserole dish or heavy-based lidded saucepan is just fine.

SERVES 4

4 tbsp olive oil
8 skinless and boneless
    chicken thighs (about
    1kg in total)
1 red onion, thinly sliced
3 garlic cloves, finely sliced
3-cm piece of fresh root
    ginger, peeled and
    finely chopped
1 Scotch bonnet chilli
    (or 2 other hot chillies),
    left whole
2 bay leaves
1 x 200g tin chopped
    tomatoes
2 tsp sweet paprika
½ tsp ground cloves
150g chunky peanut butter
250ml chicken stock
sea salt and freshly
    ground black pepper
plain brown rice, to serve

Heat the oil in a Dutchie pot, casserole or heavy lidded pan over a medium heat. Season the chicken thighs with salt and black pepper, add to the pot and brown for 5–7 minutes, turning until sealed on both sides (you may need to do this in batches). Remove and set aside.

Add the onion to the same pot and gently cook for 2–3 minutes until soft. Add the garlic, ginger, chilli and bay leaves and cook for a further 5 minutes, then add the tomatoes, paprika, cloves, peanut butter and stock and stir for a few minutes until well combined. Season to taste.

Return the chicken thighs to the pot, cover with the lid and gently simmer for 25–30 minutes, until the chicken is tender. Stir every now and then to prevent anything sticking to the base of the pot.

Check seasoning and serve with plain brown rice.

GRILLED CHICKEN ROTI WRAP WITH HOT MANGO DRESSING

Roti are really popular in the Caribbean, especially in Trinidad, where they are filled with various foods such as curries or spiced chickpeas. Here, I've used store-bought roti (or chapatis) for a quick and simple snack or a light lunch, but of course you can make your own by following my recipe on page 128.

SERVES 4

4 skinless, boneless
  chicken breasts, cut
  into strips lengthways
1 tsp cayenne pepper
1 tsp ground cumin
1 tsp smoked paprika
a pinch each of sea salt
  and black pepper
2 tbsp olive oil

**For the Hot Mango
  Dressing**
8 heaped tbsp yoghurt
3 tbsp smooth mango
  chutney
4 tsp Hot Pepper Sauce
  (see page 18 or
  store-bought)

To serve
1 x packet pre-made rotis
  (chapatis) (at least
  4 large wraps)
1 baby gem lettuce,
  leaves separated
½ red onion, finely sliced
1 avocado, sliced

Preheat the grill to its highest setting.

Place the chicken strips in a large bowl and sprinkle over the cayenne pepper, cumin, paprika, salt and pepper. Toss with your hands to ensure the chicken is well coated in the spices, then drizzle with olive oil. Place the chicken on a small baking tray and place under the hot grill, turning halfway through the cooking time, for 5–6 minutes (depending on how thick the strips are) or until cooked through.

To make the mango dressing, place all the ingredients into a small bowl and stir until well combined.

To assemble, lay the roti flat on the work surface and spoon a little of the mango dressing over each. Place a line of lettuce leaves, red onion and avocado slices down the centre of each roti and lay the chicken strips on top. Spoon over a little more dressing, then tightly roll the roti up to enclose the filling. Cut the wraps in half and enjoy.

PEPPY'S BARBECUE CHICKEN WITH JAMAICAN FRIED THYME DUMPLINGS

During my recent trip to the Caribbean, I just had to rustle up one of my mum's favourite recipes. I've added a little twist here and there over the years, but this dish always reminds me of my childhood. It's a perfect weekday supper, as it's made with lots of store cupboard and fridge ingredients.

SERVES 4

4 tbsp tomato ketchup
juice of 1 large lemon
2 tbsp soy sauce
1 tbsp dark brown sugar
1 tbsp English mustard
   powder
½ tsp ground allspice
½ tsp cayenne pepper
½ tsp sea salt
4 skinless, boneless
   chicken breasts
vegetable oil, for oiling
   pan (optional)

**For the Fried Thyme
Dumplings**
200g plain flour
1 tsp baking powder
2 tbsp finely chopped
   flat-leaf parsley
½ tsp dried thyme
½ tsp sea salt
200ml milk
vegetable oil,
   for deep-frying

To serve
mixed salad leaves
olive oil, for drizzling
freshly squeezed
   lemon juice

In a large bowl, mix together the ketchup, lemon juice, soy sauce, sugar, mustard powder, allspice, cayenne pepper and salt. Add the chicken breasts, stirring to coat in the marinade, then cover and set aside for at least 20 minutes.

Preheat a barbecue or heat an oiled griddle pan until hot.

When ready to cook, scrape off any excess marinade from the chicken and reserve.

Cook the chicken on the hot barbecue or griddle pan for 8–10 minutes on each side, until well browned and cooked through. Baste with the leftover marinade towards the end of cooking for a sticky glaze.

Meanwhile, make the dumplings. In a large bowl, mix together the flour, baking powder, herbs and salt, then beat in the milk to make a thick batter.

Fill a large deep heavy-based saucepan or wok with oil to a depth of 3cm and set over a medium-high heat. Test the oil is hot enough for deep-frying by dropping in a small piece of bread: it should sizzle and brown in 40–50 seconds. Carefully drop heaped tablespoonfuls of the dumpling batter into the hot oil and fry for 3–4 minutes until golden brown, puffed up and cooked through. Don't overcrowd the pan – cook no more than a few at a time. Remove with a slotted spoon to drain on kitchen paper.

Serve the barbecued chicken with the fried dumplings, accompanied by mixed salad leaves drizzled with olive oil and lemon juice.

POPPY & COCONUT BEEF KEBABS WITH ROASTED CHILLI SALSA

These kebabs are lovely to cook on the barbecue, but are just as good made on a chargrill pan if the weather isn't ideal. The toasted coconut adds a nutty sweetness to this spicy dish.

SERVES 4

1kg beef sirloin,
  cut into 2½cm dice
3 tbsp olive oil
2 tbsp minced garlic
2 tbsp minced ginger
1 tsp dried red chilli flakes
3 tbsp poppy seeds
3 tbsp white sesame seeds
1 tbsp cumin seeds
4 tbsp desiccated coconut

For the Roasted Chilli Salsa
3 long green chillies,
  tops trimmed
6–8 tbsp extra-virgin olive
  oil, plus an extra drizzle
  for oiling the chillies
1 garlic clove, peeled
a large handful of
  flat-leaf parsley
a handful of mint
juice of 1 lemon
sea salt and freshly
  ground black pepper

Preheat a barbecue (if using).

Place the diced beef in a large bowl. In a separate small bowl, mix together the olive oil, garlic and ginger and pour over the beef. Mix with your hands to ensure the beef is well coated. Cover the bowl with clingfilm and marinate in the fridge for 1 hour.

Next, make the salsa. Unless using a barbecue, preheat the grill to its highest setting.

Place the green chillies on a small baking tray and lightly drizzle with oil. Place the tray under the hot grill for 5–10 minutes, until the chillies are charred and blistered – they should be nice and soft. Alternatively, this can be done directly on the barbecue.

Put the garlic, parsley, mint, lemon juice and charred chillies into a food processor and pulse for 4–5 seconds. Add the oil and pulse again, until the mixture is well combined but still quite coarse. Season with salt and pepper and set aside.

Heat a small dry frying pan over a low heat, add the chilli flakes, poppy seeds, sesame seeds, cumin seeds and desiccated coconut and lightly toast. As soon as the coconut turns golden, remove from the heat and tip into a pestle and mortar. Grind to a coarse texture.

Remove the marinated beef from the fridge, add the spice mixture and massage the spices into the beef. Thread the pieces of beef onto skewers.

Place the beef skewers on the barbecue (or on a pre-heated chargrill pan) and grill, turning frequently, for about 6 minutes, depending on how you like your beef cooked. Once cooked, remove from the heat and let rest for 5 minutes before serving.

To serve, place the beef kebabs on a board and spoon over the salsa.

PORKY PUMPKIN & RED BEAN RUNDOWN

Porky Pumpkin – I know, it sounds like a cartoon character, but it really is a delicious meal! During cooking, it fills the kitchen with the amazing aroma of Caribbean spices. Mmmm.

SERVES 4

2 tbsp olive oil
1kg pork cheeks,
    cut into 3cm dice
2 white onions, finely diced
2 garlic cloves, crushed
4-cm piece of fresh root
    ginger, grated
1 small Scotch bonnet
    chilli, whole
4 fresh thyme sprigs
1 cinnamon stick
1 tsp ground cloves
1 tsp ground allspice
600ml chicken stock
1 x 400ml tin coconut milk
300g pumpkin or butternut
    squash, peeled, de-seeded
    and roughly diced
1 x 400g tin red beans,
    drained and rinsed
juice of 1 lime
a handful of chopped
    fresh coriander
Clap-hand Roti (page 128)
    or steamed rice, to serve

Preheat the oven to 180°C/160°C fan/gas 4.

Heat the oil in a large flameproof casserole dish with a lid, set over a high heat. Add the diced pork cheeks and brown in batches, making sure not to overcrowd the pan. Remove and set aside.

Reduce the heat and add the onions to the same pan. Gently cook for about 3–4 minutes, until softened, then add the garlic, ginger, chilli, thyme sprigs, cinnamon stick, cloves and allspice and cook for 30 seconds, just to remove the rawness of the spice. Return the browned pork cheeks to the pan and coat well with the spices. Pour in the stock and coconut milk and bring to a simmer, then cover with the lid and transfer the casserole dish to the oven to cook for 40 minutes.

Remove the casserole from the oven and add the pumpkin or squash and red beans. Carefully stir together, cover with the lid and return to the oven for a further 30–40 minutes, until the meat and pumpkin are tender.

To finish, stir through the lime juice and coriander and serve with Clap-hand Roti (page 128) or steamed rice.

RUM & SWEET MUSTARD RIBEYE STEAK

This is my version of a delicious steak recipe I tried in the Caribbean. It's a simple, quick marinade and the sweetened rum and mustard work brilliantly with the beef. Ribeye steak is great to use for this, but you can choose the cut of your choice and alter the cooking times accordingly.

SERVES 4

100ml dark rum
100ml dark soy sauce
100g light brown sugar
2 tbsp Dijon mustard
½ tsp freshly crushed
    peppercorns
2 x 500g ribeye steaks
green salad and chips
    (optional), to serve

In a small bowl, combine the rum, soy sauce, brown sugar, mustard and crushed peppercorns and mix together until the sugar has dissolved. Place the steaks in a shallow dish and pour the marinade over the top. Set aside to marinate at room temperature for at least 30 minutes.

Preheat a barbecue or chargrill pan until hot.

Remove the steak from the marinade, shaking off the excess and reserving the marinade. Grill the steaks for 3 minutes until good char marks appear, then rotate the meat by 90 degrees to get a cross-hatch effect and continue grilling for another 3 minutes. Turn the steak over and repeat on the other side, until cooked to your liking (10–12 minutes in total for medium-rare). Set aside to rest for 5 minutes before slicing.

Meanwhile, put the marinade into a small saucepan set over a medium-high heat, bring to the boil and cook for 3–4 minutes until reduced and syrupy.

Slice the steaks thinly across the grain. Serve drizzled with the sweet mustard sauce, with a simple green salad... and perhaps some chips!

SPICED SPATCHCOCK CHICKEN WITH PAPAYA GLAZE

The papaya, sometimes known as the paw paw, is a nutritious tropical fruit with a sweet and musky taste. In the Caribbean, it's often used in savoury dishes, especially when unripe. The fruit and leaves of the papaya contain an enzyme that actually helps to tenderise meat, so it's great to use in marinades. The flavour it adds to this sticky, sweet glaze works brilliantly with the spices.

SERVES 4

1 x 1.5kg chicken, backbone removed and spatchcocked (ask your butcher to do this)
1 tbsp ground allspice
1 tbsp smoked paprika
2 tbsp olive oil
a handful of watercress, to serve

For the Papaya Glaze
2 tbsp olive oil
½ white onion, finely chopped
1 tsp chilli flakes
500g papaya, peeled and diced
200g caster sugar
150ml water
80ml white wine vinegar
a pinch of salt

First, marinate the spatchcocked chicken. Place the chicken on a large tray and sprinkle over the spices. Massage the spices into the skin and meat, then cover with clingfilm and place in the fridge for at least 2 hours, or preferably overnight.

To make the glaze, heat the oil in a saucepan set on a medium heat, add the onion and chilli flakes and cook for 3–4 minutes, until soft. Add the diced papaya, sugar, water, vinegar and salt, bring to the boil and cook until reduced by half. Transfer the mixture to a blender and blend until smooth, then pour into a bowl and set aside.

Preheat a barbecue or oven to 200°C/180°C fan/gas 6.

Remove the marinated chicken from the fridge and feed two skewers through the thickest part of the chicken in a cross shape – this holds the chicken together and makes it easier to handle. Drizzle with olive oil and place the chicken on the hot barbecue grill, skin-side up. Grill for 20–25 minutes, moving it around frequently, then flip the chicken over to crisp up the skin for a further 10–15 minutes, making sure the skin doesn't burn. When the skin is crisp, turn the chicken over and baste with the papaya glaze. Repeat this process on both sides for 10 minutes so that it is well glazed. Test to see if the chicken is cooked through by inserting a small knife into the thickest part of the leg – if the juices run clear, it is done. Remove from the heat and let rest for 10–15 minutes. Alternatively, roast the chicken in the hot oven for 30 minutes at 200°C/180°C fan/gas 6 and then increase the heat to 220°C/200°C fan/gas 7 and roast for a further 10–15 minutes until the chicken skin is crispy and the juices run clear.

Cut the chicken into pieces, pop onto a wooden board, sprinkle with watercress and serve.

TAMARIND TREACLE & RUM-GLAZED RIBS

Tender baby back ribs that fall off the bone... there's nothing better. Basting keeps them moist and succulent and the tamarind delivers that gorgeous sweet-and-sour taste. These glazed ribs are great served with my Spiced Buttered Corn-on-the-Cob, a summer favourite in my house.

SERVES 4

6 tbsp black treacle
5 tbsp tamarind paste
250ml dark rum
4 large garlic cloves, crushed
2 red chillies, finely chopped
1 tsp chilli powder
1 tsp black mustard seeds
2 tsp black pepper
2 tsp sea salt
2 x 650–700g baby back
   pork rib racks

**For the Spiced Buttered
   Corn-on-the-Cob**
150g butter, softened
2 tsp smoked paprika
1 tsp ground allspice
1 tsp chilli flakes
2 garlic cloves, crushed
1 tsp salt
1 tsp black pepper
4 corn cobs, in their husks

In a large mixing bowl, whisk together the black treacle, tamarind paste, rum, garlic, chillies, chilli powder, black mustard seeds, pepper and salt.

Place the ribs in a deep roasting tray and pour over the marinade. Roll the ribs around in the marinade to ensure they are well covered, then cover with clingfilm and place in the fridge for at least 2 hours, or preferably overnight.

Preheat the oven to 200°C/180°C fan/gas 6.

Remove the ribs from the fridge and allow to come up to room temperature.

Remove the clingfilm, re-cover the roasting tray with foil and place in the oven for 30 minutes.

To make the Spiced Buttered Corn-on-the-Cob, mix together the butter, paprika, allspice, chilli flakes, garlic, salt and pepper.

Take the corn cobs and carefully peel back the husks, but do not completely remove. Remove any corn silk (this is the yellow stringy part of the corn around the husks). Liberally spread the smoky, spiced butter all over the corn, then roll back the husks to cover and tightly wrap each one in foil.

Pop the ribs into the hot oven. After 30 minutes remove the foil from the tray and spoon over the juices from the bottom of the tray to baste the ribs. Return the ribs to the oven and repeat this process once or twice more while cooking for a further 45 minutes until the ribs are well-glazed, sticky and tender – the meat should readily ease away from the bone. Let rest for 10–12 minutes before serving.

Place the cobs on a baking tray and roast in the oven for 25–30 minutes. Alternatively, place them straight onto a barbecue and grill for 25–30 minutes, turning from time to time.

To serve, unwrap the corn cobs, discarding the foil. The husks will come away easily, revealing the ready-to-eat corn. Serve the ribs with the corn alongside. Get licking those fingers.

WATERFALL PORK BELLY
WITH ISLAND PROVISIONS

I'm serving this tender, succulent pork and its crispy crackling with traditional Caribbean provisions. Traditionally, 'ground provisions' is the term used to describe local root vegetables, such as yams, cassava, sweet potatoes, dasheen and plantain. You can use any combination you like and I recommend you trying to get hold of dasheen for its slightly nutty flavour. This makes a great Sunday lunch with a difference.

SERVES 4

1.5kg pork belly, skin on
4 tbsp cider vinegar
4 tbsp butter
6 garlic cloves, crushed
6 bay leaves, crushed
2 tbsp sea salt
1 tbsp crushed black
    peppercorns
300ml white wine
300ml chicken stock

For the root vegetables
1 yam, peeled and
    roughly chopped
1 dasheen, peeled and
    roughly chopped
1 sweet potato, peeled
    and roughly chopped
2 parsnips, cut lengthways
    into wedges
2 red onions, cut
    into wedges
4 garlic cloves
12 new potatoes
4 thyme sprigs
1 tbsp olive oil
250ml cold water

Bring a kettle of water to the boil. Place the pork in a colander, skin-side up, and carefully pour the boiling water over the pork rind. Let cool slightly, then rub the pork all over with cider vinegar, place it on a plate, cover and chill in the fridge overnight.

Preheat the oven to 200°C/180°C fan/gas 6.

In a bowl, blend together the butter, garlic, crushed bay leaves, salt and pepper, then spread it over the pork, ensuring it is thoroughly covered.

Place the pork, skin-side up, on a wire rack over an empty roasting pan (or on the oven shelf above), so that any juices can drip down into the pan. Roast for 1 hour.

Reduce the oven temperature to 180°C/160°C fan/gas 4.

Remove the pan with the pork juices from the oven and add the prepared vegetables, thyme, olive oil and water. Place the vegetable pan back underneath the pork and roast for a further 1 hour, basting the vegetables with the juices in the pan from time to time.

Take the pork from the oven and set aside to rest for 15 minutes. Remove the vegetables from the roasting pan with a slotted spoon and keep warm. Drain off any fat in the pan, leaving just the cooking juices behind.

To make the gravy, set the pan with the cooking juices over a medium heat, add the wine and stock and bring to the boil, then cook until the liquid has reduced by half. Strain through a sieve and skim off any fat.

Remove the crackling from the pork in one piece, carve the pork and serve with the crackling, roasted vegetables and gravy.

PEPPY'S BRAISED OXTAIL WITH BUTTERBEANS

Once seen as a cheap cut, oxtail is now celebrated by chefs around the world. Although it can be tough, when it's cooked slowly it breaks down into a soft and flavoursome, beefy delight. I've always loved this dish and the heavenly aroma of it cooking still reminds me of my childhood. It's rich and hearty and perfect for a lazy Sunday with family and friends.

SERVES 4

50g plain flour
1 tbsp cayenne pepper
1.5kg oxtail pieces
4 tbsp olive oil
2 white onions,
    finely chopped
2 celery sticks, peeled
    and de-stringed,
    finely chopped
2 garlic cloves,
    finely chopped
½ Scotch bonnet chilli,
    finely chopped
3 thyme sprigs
2–3 bay leaves
1 tbsp tomato purée
300ml red wine
1 litre chicken stock
1 x 400g tin chopped
    tomatoes
1 tbsp Worcestershire sauce
2 x 400g tins butterbeans,
    drained and rinsed
a handful of flat-leaf
    parsley, chopped
sea salt and freshly
    ground black pepper
steamed white rice,
    to serve

Put the flour into a large bowl and season with a large pinch of salt and the cayenne pepper. Add the oxtail pieces, tossing to ensure the meat is thoroughly covered with the flour.

Heat the oil in a large flameproof casserole or Dutchie pot over a high heat and brown the oxtail pieces on all sides (in batches if necessary). Using tongs, transfer to a colander over a bowl and allow the excess oil to drain off.

Add the onions and celery to the same pan and sauté for 5–6 minutes until softened. Stir in the garlic, chilli, thyme, bay leaves and tomato purée and cook for 1–2 minutes. Deglaze the pan with the red wine, scraping the bottom of the pan to release any caramelised juices, then pour in the chicken stock, tomatoes and Worcestershire sauce. Season with a pinch each of salt and pepper.

Return the oxtail to the pan, bring to the boil, then cover and gently simmer over a low heat for 1½ hours, skimming if and when needed. Gently stir in the butterbeans and continue to cook for a further 20–30 minutes, until the meat just starts to come away from the bone and the beans are tender.

Sprinkle with parsley and serve with steamed white rice if you like.

GRILLED LAMB CUTLETS WITH FRESH HERBY GREEN YOGHURT

Lamb is one of my favourite meats. I especially like barbecued or chargrilled cutlets, because the bone gives you a natural handle to eat them with. Dipped into my herby green yoghurt, these could become one of your favourites too! You can also cook them under a hot grill.

SERVES 4

zest of 2 limes
1 tbsp finely grated
    fresh root ginger
1 tsp curry powder
1 tsp chilli powder
2 tbsp olive oil
750g lamb cutlets
sea salt and freshly
    ground black pepper

**For the Herby Green
    Yoghurt**
1 x 170g tub natural yoghurt
1 green chilli, de-seeded
    and finely chopped
1 garlic clove, finely
    chopped or grated
1 tbsp finely grated
    fresh root ginger
a handful of mint leaves,
    roughly chopped
a handful of coriander,
    roughly chopped
a handful of flat-leaf parsley,
    roughly chopped
juice of 1 lime
sea salt and freshly
    ground black pepper

In a large bowl, mix together the lime zest, ginger, curry powder, chilli powder and olive oil. Season with salt and pepper and mix well. Add the lamb cutlets and toss through the marinade, ensuring they are well coated. Set aside to marinate for 30 minutes.

To make the herby green yoghurt, put the yoghurt into a bowl and add the chilli, garlic, ginger, herbs and lime juice. Give everything a good mix together and season to taste.

Preheat the barbecue or a chargrill pan to medium–high.

Cook the cutlets on the barbecue or in the chargrill pan for 4–5 minutes on each side (depending on how you like your lamb cooked). Once cooked, remove from the heat and let rest for a couple of minutes.

To serve, lay the cutlets on a board, drizzle over some of the herby green yoghurt and serve the remainder in a bowl on the side for dipping.

BUTTERMILK CHICKEN BURGERS WITH TAMARIND MAYONNAISE

There are some fantastic green seasonings on the market, so by all means use one of these, but it really is worth making your own if you can – the freshness of the herbs really adds an extra something. Any leftover seasoning can be kept – I freeze mine in an ice-cube tray for convenience. Toss with root vegetables, add to curries or homemade soups for a spicy dash.

SERVES 4

For the Green Seasoning
a large handful each of flat-
    leaf parsley and coriander
1 tbsp fresh thyme leaves
2 green Scotch bonnet
    chillies
2 garlic cloves, halved
1 shallot, roughly chopped
4 spring onions,
    roughly chopped
2 tbsp olive oil
sea salt and freshly ground
    black pepper, to taste

For the Buttermilk Chicken
300ml buttermilk
2 tbsp Scotch bonnet green
    seasoning (see above)
4 large boneless skinless
    chicken thighs
vegetable oil, for deep-frying
100g plain flour
2 eggs, beaten
150g panko breadcrumbs

**For the Tamarind
    Mayonnaise**
5 tbsp mayonnaise
1 tbsp tamarind paste
1 tbsp tomato ketchup
a splash of hot pepper sauce
1 garlic clove, minced

To serve
4 ciabatta buns
1 baby gem lettuce, leaves
    separated, washed

To make the green seasoning, place all the ingredients into a food processor and blitz together until smooth.

For the buttermilk chicken, mix together the buttermilk and green seasoning in a large bowl, add the chicken thighs and stir until they are well coated. Cover and place in the fridge for 2–3 hours, or ideally overnight, to tenderise and marinate.

Meanwhile, make the tamarind mayonnaise. Mix together all of the ingredients in a small bowl. Taste for sharpness and heat and adjust according to how you like it. Cover and chill until needed.

Fill a large deep heavy-based saucepan with vegetable oil to a depth of 4cm and set over a medium–high heat. Test the oil is hot enough for deep-frying by dropping in a small piece of bread: it should sizzle and brown in 40–50 seconds.

Meanwhile, place the flour in a large bowl, place the eggs in a separate large bowl and the panko breadcrumbs into a third. Remove the chicken from the fridge and brush off any excess buttermilk marinade. Dip each chicken thigh into the flour, then into the egg and finally into the breadcrumbs, coating well. Carefully lower each chicken thigh into the hot oil and cook for 7–8 minutes until golden, carefully turning the chicken with tongs to ensure they don't stick together (you can cook in batches, if easier). Remove to drain on kitchen paper.

Slice the buns in half and lightly toast.

Spread 1 tablespoon of the tamarind mayonnaise over the base of each bun, then place baby gem leaves on top, add a crispy chicken thigh and a little more of the mayo, before topping with the other half of the bun.

CHICKEN CALYPSO

This is one of the classic dishes of Dominica. It's rich and full of flavour and, although there are many variations, it typically consists of chicken breast or thighs with vegetables and cashew nuts stewed with spices. It's traditionally served with cassava bread, but I like to serve mine over steamed rice.

SERVES 4

4 skinless chicken breasts
3 tbsp olive oil
4 tbsp guava jelly
1 onion, finely sliced
2½-cm piece of fresh root ginger, finely julienned
150g button mushrooms, sliced
100g unsalted cashew nuts, roasted
200ml red wine
200ml chicken stock
1 tbsp cornflour, mixed with 3 tbsp water
steamed rice, to serve

For the marinade
4 tbsp white wine vinegar
2 tbsp sugar
2 garlic cloves, grated
2 thyme sprigs
1 tsp ground allspice
a good grating of fresh nutmeg
1 tsp crushed black peppercorns
1 tsp sea salt

To make the marinade, combine all the ingredients in a large bowl. Score the chicken breasts, place them in the marinade and mix until thoroughly coated. Cover with clingfilm and marinate for 2–3 hours or overnight in the fridge.

Heat 2 tablespoons of the oil in a large frying pan over a medium heat. Remove the chicken from the marinade and brush off any excess. Carefully place the chicken in the hot pan and seal the meat on all sides. Add the guava jelly to the pan and let it melt and bubble down, then use tongs to turn the chicken breast in the hot glaze until lightly brown. Remove from the pan and set aside.

Meanwhile, heat the remaining tablespoon of oil in a saucepan over a medium heat, add the onions and ginger and cook for 2 minutes until softened. Add the mushrooms and sauté for 3–4 minutes, then stir through the cashews.

Increase the heat under the chicken pan and deglaze with the red wine. Add the stock and bring to a boil, then whisk in the slaked cornflour. Add the mushroom mixture, then return the chicken to the pan. Cover and cook for 20 minutes, until the chicken is cooked through and tender and the sauce has reduced to a dark, shiny and rich consistency.

Serve over steamed rice.

PORK MEDALLIONS WITH A RUM, CREAM & NUTMEG SAUCE

Nutmeg is the national symbol of Grenada and its tree grows all over the island. It's almost impossible not to taste nutmeg's distinctive flavour when visiting the so-called Spice Island – it's added to cocktails, cocoa, ice-cream, pastries and sauces. In this dish, which I made overlooking the beautiful True Blue Bay, the nutmeg sauce adds a slightly sweet, warm flavour that perfectly complements the tender pork. You can use a combination of sweet potato and pumpkin for the mash, if you like.

SERVES 4

2 tbsp olive oil
1-2 pork tenderloins
    (about 800g), trimmed
    and cut into 8 medallions
sea salt and freshly ground
    black pepper
200g pak choi, lightly
    steamed to serve

For the Sweet Potato Mash
3 large sweet potatoes
    (about 750g), peeled
2 tbsp unsalted butter
a pinch of freshly
    grated nutmeg
sea salt and freshly
    ground black pepper

**For the Rum, Cream
    and Nutmeg Sauce**
1 tbsp unsalted butter
1 shallot, finely chopped
25ml dark rum
250ml chicken stock
100ml double cream
1 tsp freshly grated nutmeg
sea salt and freshly
    ground black pepper

Put the sweet potatoes into a large pan of water, bring to the boil, then reduce the heat and simmer for 10–12 minutes, or until the potatoes are tender when pierced with a fork. Drain well, then return to the pan and mash until smooth. Add the butter and nutmeg and season with some salt and pepper.

Meanwhile, place a large frying pan over a high heat and add the olive oil. Season the pork with salt and pepper, then carefully place into the hot pan and brown until sealed all over. Reduce the heat and cook for a further 6–8 minutes, turning occasionally. Remove to a plate and keep warm.

Make the sauce in the same pan; add the butter and shallot and cook for a few minutes until softened. Deglaze the pan with the rum and carefully flambé to burn off the alcohol. Add the chicken stock and bring to the boil, then cook until the mixture has reduced by two-thirds. Add the cream and any juices from the rested pork medallions, bring back to the boil, and cook until thickened to a double cream consistency. To finish the sauce, add the grated nutmeg and check the seasoning.

To serve, place a large spoonful of the sweet potato mash on one side of each plate, lay the pork medallions next to the mash, then spoon over the sauce and serve with pak choi.

DESSERTS

LIME-GLAZED PINEAPPLE WITH PASSION FRUIT VANILLA CREAM

The pineapples in the Caribbean are sublime. If you've been lucky enough to try an Antigua Black pineapple you will know what I am talking about – they are said to be the world's sweetest pineapple and they are just delicious. This is a simple, tasty recipe that lets the pineapple take centre stage; the size of the fruit will dictate the size or number of the servings.

SERVES 6

1 medium ripe pineapple
100g apricot jam
zest and juice of 1 lime
1 tsp whole black
    peppercorns

**For the Passion Fruit
    Vanilla Cream**
2 large passion fruit
150ml double cream
25g caster sugar
½ tsp vanilla extract

Without removing the skin or top of the pineapple, slice lengthways all the way through the pineapple (including through the leaves of the top) to create 6 wedges and remove the core.

In a small pan, heat the apricot jam, lime zest and juice and peppercorns over a medium heat for about 3–4 minutes until the jam has melted. Set aside.

To make the passion fruit cream, cut each passion fruit in half, scoop out the pulp and pass through a fine sieve into a bowl, pushing the pulp down firmly to release all the juices. Reserve 1 tablespoon of the seeds.

In a separate bowl, whisk together the cream, sugar and vanilla extract, then slowly add the passion fruit juice to the cream until well combined. Gently stir in the reserved passion fruit seeds. Place in the fridge to chill.

Meanwhile, preheat a barbecue or a chargrill pan until hot.

Cook the pineapple wedges on the grill or chargrill pan until char marks appear, 2–3 minutes on each side. Brush with the apricot and lime glaze and rotate a couple of times, so that the glaze caramelises all over the surface of the pineapple.

Remove the pineapple wedges from the heat and serve immediately with a generous helping of the passion fruit cream.

BANANA TARTE TATIN WITH SPICED RUM CREAM

This is my island twist on a classic tarte Tatin. The spices and rum add a real taste of the Caribbean and it's an indulgent dessert that's great for a dinner party. You can serve this hot or cold, but straight from the oven is wonderful as you really get to enjoy the soft caramel and banana juices.

SERVES 4–6

6 large bananas
juice of ½ orange
¼ tsp ground allspice
175g golden caster sugar
60g unsalted butter, cubed
225g ready-rolled puff pastry
plain flour, for dusting

For the Spiced Rum Cream
200ml double cream
1 tbsp icing sugar
splash of dark rum
½ tsp grated nutmeg
½ tsp ground cinnamon
zest of 1 orange

Preheat oven to 200°C/180°C fan/gas 6.

Meanwhile, peel the bananas, cut into thick slices, place in a bowl and toss in half of the orange juice and the allspice. Set aside.

In a 24-cm heavy-based ovenproof frying pan, without stirring, gently heat the sugar over a low heat until dissolved and then turn the heat up to medium–high and cook for 1–2 minutes until the sugar turns a golden caramel colour. If necessary, gently move the pan but do not stir. Remove from the heat. Gradually add the cubed butter, stirring to combine, until the mixture looks like a thick, glossy caramel.

Place the cut bananas in the pan in a circle nestled into the caramel.

Open out the pastry on a lightly dusted work surface and use a rolling pin to roll it out into a circle just bigger than the frying pan and about 2½cm thick. Place the pastry on top of the pan and roughly tuck in the edges with a fork (so that when the tarte is turned out, it will hold in the caramel).

Transfer the pan to the oven and bake for 20–25 minutes, until the pastry is risen and golden brown.

Meanwhile, make the spiced rum cream. Whisk the double cream with the icing sugar until soft peaks form, then add the rum, nutmeg, cinnamon and orange zest, and whisk gently until combined.

Remove the tarte from the oven and let rest for no more than 2 minutes, then loosen the edges with a blunt knife. Place a large plate on top of the pan and, in one swift movement, invert the tarte onto the plate. Cut into slices and serve with a dollop of the spiced rum cream.

WARM TROPICAL FRUITS IN SPICED RUM WITH COCONUT ICE CREAM

Spicy, boozy and zesty tropical fruits with creamy coconut ice cream? Yes please! Keep the Scotch bonnet chilli whole, so that you get the flavour but only a gentle heat – the seeds would make the dish too hot. I'm serving the fruits with my coconut ice cream, but I won't tell you off if you use a store-bought one!

SERVES 4

500ml pink grapefruit juice
350g golden caster sugar
4 cloves
1 cinnamon stick
1 star anise
zest of 1 lime, peeled
    with a vegetable peeler
1 small slice of fresh
    root ginger
1 small Scotch bonnet
    chilli, whole
150ml golden rum
1 pineapple, peeled
    and diced
1 mango, peeled and diced
1 papaya, peeled and diced
1 dragon fruit, cut in
    half, flesh scooped
    out and diced

For the Coconut Ice Cream
1 x 400ml tin coconut milk
4 medium egg yolks
75g caster sugar
200ml double cream

First, make the coconut ice cream. Pour the coconut milk into a non-stick (or other non-reactive) saucepan and slowly bring to the boil.

Whisk the egg yolks and sugar together in a bowl until pale and creamy, then whisk in the hot coconut milk. Return the mixture to the pan and cook over a gentle heat, stirring, until it coats the back of a wooden spoon. Pour the mixture into a shallow plastic container, stir in the double cream and leave to cool. Cover and chill in the fridge for 1 hour.

Pour the chilled mixture into an ice cream machine and churn until frozen, according to the manufacturer's instructions.

Meanwhile, combine the pink grapefruit juice, sugar, cloves, cinnamon stick, star anise, lime zest, ginger and the whole chilli in a large saucepan and set over a medium heat. Bring to a simmer and cook for 3–4 minutes to infuse and dissolve the sugar. Reduce the heat, remove the chilli and add the rum, followed by the pineapple, mango, papaya and dragon fruit. Gently cook for 10 minutes, stirring occasionally to make sure that the fruit is submerged. Remove from the heat and allow the fruit to cool slightly in the syrup before serving.

Spoon the fruit and syrup into small serving bowls and serve warm with the coconut ice cream.

THE SPICE ISLANDS

Caribbean food is famously spicy – it doesn't have to be too hot, but the flavour of spice is always there. Some spices, such as allspice and chilli, are native to the islands, but others were cultivated by Asian and African migrants. Now, herbs and spices grow in abundance. They not only provide flavour, but give colour and variety to Caribbean cuisine.

Perhaps the most important spice in Caribbean cooking is allspice or pimento, as it is otherwise known. It's not actually a mix of spices as its name suggests, but a single spice from the dried fruit berry of the pimento tree. It has a potent flavour and a sweet taste, like a combination of cinnamon, nutmeg, cloves and pepper, hence its name. In Creole cooking, allspice is used frequently to season seafood dishes. Allspice leaves can be used like bay leaves and are often dropped into stews. The ground spice is a main component of jerk seasoning and it provides depth of flavour to this famous Jamaican dish.

Ginger is another spice not originally native to the Caribbean, but the tropical climate is perfect for its cultivation. Jamaican ginger is now known as some of the best in the world. It gives a zesty taste to island dishes such as jerk, ginger cake and, of course, ginger beer.

Nutmeg, originally brought over from Indonesia, is now cultivated in the Caribbean. Grenada is the second-largest exporter of nutmeg in the world. Dried in its shell for three months, the nut is then grated for use. Freshly grated nutmeg is used to flavour sauces and savoury dishes, as well as desserts and drinks – particularly eggnog and rum punch.

Cinnamon adds a fragrant warmth to meat dishes, desserts and drinks. Cloves have been used for both medicinal and culinary purposes for centuries and are an important ingredient in jerk. Garlic is an essential ingredient in Caribbean cooking, especially in jerk and fish dishes. Garlic is said to have many health benefits, helping to prevent viruses and reducing blood pressure, for example. Indigenous to Africa, tamarind is now cultivated in the Caribbean and used as a flavouring in many dishes. It's actually the pulp from a fruit pod that is used in cooking to provide a sweet and sour tangy taste.

Not strictly a 'spice', but an important part of Caribbean spice seasoning is the Scotch bonnet chilli pepper. Used frequently in local cooking, it is added to jerk, curried goat, chow and fish dishes. It's one of the hottest peppers in the world, but when used sparingly it adds a delicious sweet yet savoury taste to sauces.

Also worth mentioning is thyme. Originally from the Mediterranean, this aromatic herb is now an integral ingredient in Caribbean cuisine. Used to add a fragrant, punchy flavour, the herb is one of the trinity of Jamaican cooking (Scotch bonnet, spring onion and thyme), which forms the base of traditional dishes, including rice 'n' peas.

There are so many more spices I could talk about, such as turmeric and coriander (chadon beni), used in Indian- and Asian-influenced dishes, but the above are the most frequently used in Caribbean cuisine. You can buy ready-mixed Caribbean seasonings, such as 'green seasoning', Bajan seasoning or jerk, but try making your own selection (see page 106) to instantly add flavour and zing to your fish, meat and vegetable dishes.

BUTTER RUM CAKE

This butter rum cake was made for me in the Caribbean and I just had to recreate it when I returned home. It's quite possibly the best rum cake ever! It calls for a packet of instant vanilla pudding, which is quite usual in the Caribbean and America, but not so easy to get hold of here. You can use instant custard powder or an instant dessert mix like butterscotch Angel Delight, instead. Yes, I know it sounds strange – but it really does work!

MAKES 8–10 SLICES

125g unsalted butter, plus extra for greasing the tin
250g self-raising flour, plus extra for flouring the tin
60g walnuts, chopped
30g cornflour
3 tsp baking powder
1 tsp salt
4 eggs
200ml whole milk
200ml dark rum
1 tbsp vanilla extract
6 tbsp vegetable oil
300g granulated sugar
1 x 75g packet instant vanilla pudding mix
crème fraîche or ice cream, to serve

For the rum syrup
125g unsalted butter
75ml water
150g granulated sugar
a good pinch of salt
100ml dark rum

Preheat the oven to 180°C/160°C fan/gas 4.

Grease and flour a 27-cm bundt pan or fluted cake tin and sprinkle the bottom with the chopped walnuts.

In a large bowl, combine the self-raising flour, cornflour, baking powder and salt.

In a separate bowl, whisk together the eggs, milk, rum, vanilla extract and 3 tablespoons of the vegetable oil.

Cream the sugar and butter in a food mixer fitted with a balloon whisk until pale and fluffy. Slowly add the dry ingredients and the remaining 3 tablespoons of vegetable oil and continue to mix for a few minutes on a medium-low speed, until the mixture looks like sand. Add the instant pudding mix and the egg mixture, scraping any mixture from the sides back down into the bowl with a spatula, and mix again on medium speed until well combined. The cake batter should be thin and smooth.

Pour the batter into the bundt tin and bake for 50–60 minutes, until an inserted skewer comes out clean.

Meanwhile, make the rum syrup. In a saucepan set over a medium-high heat, combine the butter, water, sugar and salt and cook, stirring, until the butter has melted and the sugar has dissolved. Bring to the boil, then reduce the heat to low and simmer for 10 minutes. Remove from the heat and slowly stir in the rum. Set aside to cool.

Remove the cake from the oven and let it rest in the tin for 10 minutes. Loosen the cake slightly from the tin (inverting it onto a plate works best), then place it back in the tin. Poke several holes into the top of the cake with a skewer to help the syrup seep in, then slowly pour half of the rum syrup over the cake. Let it stand for 15–20 minutes, then invert onto a serving platter and slowly pour the remaining syrup over the cake until it is all absorbed.

Serve with a dollop of crème fraîche or ice cream. Delicious and naughty... enjoy!

CARAMEL PLUM SUNDAE WITH PINK PEPPERCORN NUT BRITTLE

This is a rather grown-up and indulgent sundae! Soft, sweet plums go perfectly with the caramel flavours and everything is lifted by a hint of spice. The brittle adds a lovely crunchy texture. You can store any brittle left over in an airtight container – it's great served with ice cream, or just to snack on!

SERVES 4

75g unsalted butter
75g caster sugar
1 cinnamon stick
1 star anise
zest and juice of 1 orange
1 vanilla pod
500g plums, quartered
   and stoned
350ml double cream
1 x 400g tin dulce de leche or
   caramel condensed milk
15g pistachios, chopped,
   to decorate

For the Pink Peppercorn Nut Brittle
15g white sesame seeds
75g pecans, roughly chopped
200g caster sugar
75g pistachios, sliced
   or chopped
1 tsp pink peppercorns,
   crushed

Melt the butter and caster sugar in a large saucepan set over a medium heat, until the sugar has dissolved, then add the cinnamon stick, star anise, orange zest and juice. Split the vanilla pod, scrape it with a knife to release the seeds and add the pod and seeds to the pan. Stir to combine, then add the plums, reduce the heat and simmer until the plums break down into a purée, about 10–12 minutes. Remove the cinnamon stick, star anise and vanilla pod, then transfer the mixture to a food processor and blend until smooth. Pass the plum purée through a fine sieve into a bowl and leave to cool.

To make the brittle, toast the sesame seeds in a dry non-stick frying pan over a low heat, until golden, then set aside. Toast the pecans in the same way and set aside. Place the sugar into the same pan and cook over a low heat until the sugar has dissolved and formed a light golden caramel. Take the pan off the heat and quickly stir in the sesame seeds, pecans, pistachios and pink peppercorns, ensuring they are well coated. Turn the mixture out onto a heatproof mat, spread evenly and leave to set.

In a large bowl, lightly whisk the double cream to soft peaks, then add the dulce de leche and gently whisk together until firm. Spoon 2–3 tablespoons of the plum purée into the caramel cream and ripple through. Place in the fridge for 20 minutes to chill.

Divide the remaining plum purée equally among tall sundae glasses and spoon the chilled caramel plum cream on top.

Break up the nutty brittle into small shards and place them on top of the sundaes. To finish, grate some of the brittle over the sundaes and add a sprinkling of chopped pistachios for extra crunch.

COCONUT WATER & RUM PUNCH GRANITA WITH LIME SYRUP

Sit in your back garden or open your windows on a bright sunny day, put on some music and relax with this refreshing Coconut and Rum Punch Granita. You'll be taken to the shores of the Caribbean with the first mouthful!

SERVES 4

350ml coconut water
25ml pink grapefruit juice
2–3 dashes Angostura
   bitters
1 tbsp grenadine
75ml golden rum
50ml mango juice,
   or to taste

For the Lime Syrup
zest of 1 lime
juice of 5 limes
   (150ml juice)
100g caster sugar
2 cloves
1 star anise

Whisk together the coconut water, pink grapefruit juice, bitters and grenadine in a large bowl, then add the rum and mango juice, to taste. Pour into a freezer-proof container and place in the freezer for 2 hours, after which time ice crystals should have formed. Fork through the granita, then place it back in the freezer. Repeat this process every 2 hours until completely frozen with a light and fluffy texture.

Meanwhile, make the lime syrup. Place all the ingredients into a small non-stick saucepan set over a medium heat and bring to the boil. Once the sugar has dissolved, remove from the heat and allow the cloves and star anise to infuse while it cools.

To serve, spoon the granita into Martini glasses and drizzle with the lime syrup.

190 DESSERTS

PASSION FRUIT SOUFFLÉ SHELLS WITH ZESTY PAPAYA

This is a tropical twist on one of my all-time favourites.
The addition of the papaya really adds a delicious freshness.

SERVES 4

6 large passion fruit
120ml milk
1 large egg, separated
60g caster sugar
1 tbsp plain flour
3 tbsp orange juice
1 papaya, peeled, de-seeded
    and thinly sliced
juice of 1 lime, to serve
icing sugar, for dusting

Preheat the oven to 200°C/180°C fan/gas 6.

Halve the passion fruit and scoop the flesh and seeds into a bowl.

Cut a small slice from the base of each passion fruit shell and sit them snugly in a baking dish.

In a large saucepan, gently warm the milk without boiling.

In a medium bowl and using a hand whisk, beat the egg yolk with half of the sugar until pale and light. Whisk in the flour and then the warm milk. Pour the mixture back into the pan, set over a low heat, and beat until smooth. Cook gently for 2 minutes until thickened, then remove from the heat. Stir in 3 tablespoons of the passion fruit pulp and seeds.

In a separate spotlessly clean bowl, whisk the egg white until it forms soft peaks, then add the remaining sugar and whisk to stiff peaks. Gently fold the meringue into the passion fruit custard, then divide the mixture between the passion fruit shells. Bake for 7–10 minutes until risen and golden.

Meanwhile, pass the remaining passion fruit pulp through a fine sieve into a small saucepan, add the orange juice and gently heat for 2–3 minutes, stirring until slightly thickened.

Serve the soufflés straight from the oven, placing 3 soufflé shells on each serving plate, along with the fresh papaya slices. Finish with a squeeze of lime, a drizzle of passion fruit sauce and a light dusting of icing sugar.

CHOCOLATE DROP SCONES WITH BANANA MASH-UP & FRUIT CONFETTI

When I cooked this on the beach in Saint Lucia, within minutes it was trending on social media and everyone wanted the recipe. Chocolate is big business on the island and this dessert really is the biz. I like to cut my fruit into small dice, but you can leave them slightly chunkier if you prefer.

SERVES 4–6 (MAKES 12 SMALL DROP SCONES)

For the Chocolate Drop Scones

125g self-raising flour
1 tsp baking powder
3 tbsp caster sugar
4 tbsp cocoa powder
1 large egg
175ml milk
zest of 1 orange
100g butter, melted

For the Banana Mash-Up

2–3 bananas, chopped
15g dark chocolate, grated or finely chopped
fresh nutmeg, for grating
a splash of rum (optional)

To serve

a selection of tropical fruit (I used strawberries, kiwi, papaya and pineapple), cut into small dice and tossed with a splash of coconut rum (optional)
cocoa powder, for dusting
dark chocolate shavings, to decorate

First, make the drop scone batter. Sift the flour, baking powder, sugar and cocoa powder into a large bowl. Make a well in the centre and crack in the egg. Beat the egg, while drawing in the flour. Gradually add the milk, a little at a time, slowing mixing the ingredients to form a smooth batter. Stir in the orange zest until combined.

Meanwhile, make the mash-up. Mash the bananas in a bowl with a fork, then add the chocolate and mix well. Add a grating of nutmeg, and an optional splash of rum for the adults, and mix again. Set aside.

Set a frying pan over a medium heat and spoon in a little melted butter. Add the drop scone batter to the pan 1 tablespoon at a time. Leave plenty of space between each scone, so that they don't join up. Cook until a few bubbles appear on the surface, then flip and cook for 1 minute on the other side. Add more melted butter to the pan between batches, ensuring it covers the surface fully before cooking the next batch.

To serve, stack two or three drop scones on a serving plate with a spoonful of mash-up between each layer. Finish by scattering the diced tropical fruits over the plate like confetti, dust lightly with cocoa powder and scatter over a few chocolate shavings.

MANDARIN COCONUT CREAMS WITH CRUNCHY COCONUT CRUMB

I'm always looking for something to do with mandarins and, I hope you agree, this really is the crumb!

SERVES 8

For the Mandarin Coconut Creams
5 gelatine leaves
2 x 400ml tins coconut cream
400ml whole milk
8 tbsp honey

For the sweet mandarin syrup
1 x 300g tin mandarin segments in fruit juice, drained, reserving the liquid
1 tsp vanilla bean paste
1 star anise
2 cardamom pods

Crunchy Coconut Crumb (see page 206), to decorate

Soak the gelatine leaves in cold water for 4–5 minutes to soften.

Pour the coconut cream and milk into a saucepan and bring to the boil. Remove from the heat and stir in the honey, then set aside to cool slightly.

Squeeze out the gelatine leaves and whisk them into the warm coconut cream mixture until dissolved. Pass the mixture through a fine sieve set over a jug, then set aside to settle for 5–10 minutes.

Skim off any foam that has formed on top of the mixture, then pour it evenly into small serving bowls. Cover with clingfim and place in the fridge to set for at least 4 hours, or overnight.

To make the sweet mandarin syrup, place the reserved drained mandarin syrup into a small saucepan, along with the vanilla bean paste, star anise and cardamom pods. Set over a high heat and cook until the mixture has reduced to a thick syrup. Remove from the heat and discard the star anise and cardamom. Stir through the mandarin segments and allow to cool completely.

To serve, spoon the syrupy mandarin segments on top of the chilled creams and decorate with a sprinkling of Crunchy Coconut Crumb.

WHITE CHOCOLATE, RUM & RASPBERRY CRÈME BRÛLÉE

These puddings are deliciously decadent, and the dish is elevated by the wonderful flavours of the tropics. The tang from the raspberries and the kick of rum beautifully cuts through the rich white chocolate and coconut custard.

SERVES 6

200ml coconut milk
250ml double cream
1 vanilla pod, halved and scraped to release the seeds
100g white chocolate
2 tbsp white rum
6 egg yolks
30g golden caster sugar, plus extra for sprinkling
300g fresh raspberries, mashed, plus extra whole raspberries to garnish

Preheat the oven to 180°C/160°C fan/gas 4.

Place the coconut milk, cream and the vanilla pod and its seeds in a saucepan and set over a low–medium heat. Add the white chocolate and gently heat , stirring, until the chocolate has melted. Remove from the heat, stir in the rum and set aside to infuse for 10 minutes.

In a large bowl, beat the egg yolks and sugar until pale. Pour over the hot infused cream and stir together, then strain through a fine sieve into a jug.

Bring a kettle of water to the boil.

Place six small 120ml ovenproof ramekins into a deep roasting tray and divide the mashed raspberries between them. Carry the whole tray to the oven and place inside, leaving enough space for you to access the ramekins from above – it's easier to fill the ramekins at the oven rather than carrying them when full. Carefully fill each ramekin with the cream mixture, making sure they are evenly filled. Pour enough boiling water from the kettle into the bottom of the roasting tray so that it reaches halfway up the sides of the ramekins. Bake for 20–25 minutes, until just set but still a little wobbly in the centre.

Remove the ramekins from the oven, let cool, then chill for 4 hours.

To serve, sprinkle a little golden caster sugar over each custard and caramelise with a blowtorch or place under a very hot grill until the sugar turns a dark caramel colour. Leave the caramel to harden, then serve decorated with fresh raspberries.

PINEAPPLE TOAST WITH CARAMELISED RUM BANANAS

This is a delicious, slightly boozy dessert and an absolute favourite of mine. It also makes a great brunch – it certainly gives you a kick start! I like to use a firm brioche loaf (too soft and it can go soggy in the egg mixture), but a good quality white bread works just as well. Substitute the rum with any remaining pineapple juice if you'd prefer it to be alcohol-free. My caramelised bananas are also delicious with a spoonful of clotted cream.

SERVES 4

For the Pineapple Toast
100g unsalted butter, softened
8 brioche or white bread slices, about 1cm thick
1 x 225g tin crushed pineapple
2 tsp mixed spice
2 tbsp demerara sugar
4 large eggs
1–2 tbsp dark rum
100ml single cream

For the Caramelised Rum Bananas
50g unsalted butter
3 tbsp maple syrup
1–2 tbsp dark rum
4 small bananas, peeled and cut in half on an angle
1 tbsp freshly grated coconut (optional)

To make the pineapple toast, spread half of the softened butter over one side of each of the brioche slices.

Tip the crushed pineapple into a sieve and press out all of the juice into a bowl. Spoon the pineapple into a separate bowl and stir in 1 teaspoon of the mixed spice and all of the demerara sugar.

Spoon 1 heaped tablespoon of the pineapple mixture into the centre of 4 of the brioche slices and cover with the remaining slices, buttered-side up.

In a shallow dish, beat together the eggs, rum (or pineapple juice) and remaining teaspoon of mixed spice and set aside.

Heat the remaining butter in a heavy-based frying pan set over a medium heat. Once sizzling, dip two of the pineapple sandwiches into the egg mixture until well soaked and evenly coated and carefully place into the hot pan. Cook for 2 minutes on each side until crisp and golden, then remove from the pan and repeat with the other two sandwiches.

Meanwhile, make the caramelised bananas. Set a separate large frying pan over a medium heat and add the butter. Once bubbling, add the maple syrup and stir until it begins to bubble, then add the rum and carefully flambé to burn off the alcohol (alternatively, use the pineapple juice). Add the bananas and cook for 2–3 minutes until caramelised, then flip and cook for a further 2 minutes on the other side. Add the grated coconut and serve immediately, spooned on top of the pineapple toast.

COFFEE & RUM-POACHED PEARS WITH CRUNCHY COCONUT CRUMB

Jamaican Blue Mountain Coffee is considered to be amongst the best in the world – every bean is hand inspected and it takes twice as long as other coffee to mature. I had the luxury of cooking with Blue Mountain Coffee in Jamaica, but it is quite expensive so feel free to use your favourite blend for this recipe. This is an elegant looking dessert and the gently-spiced soft pears are topped with a crunchy coconut crumb for texture.

SERVES 4

600ml freshly made
    strong filter coffee
50g brown sugar
1 star anise
4 cloves
1 cinnamon stick
75ml dark rum
4 firm dessert pears, such
    as Rocha or Comice

For the Coconut Crumb
30g plain flour
30g butter, cold, cubed
30g caster sugar
30g coconut flakes

Preheat the oven to 190°C /170°C fan/gas 5. Line a baking tray with baking parchment.

Pour the coffee into a saucepan with a lid that is large enough to hold the pears snugly, add the sugar, star anise, cloves, cinnamon and rum and heat gently over a low heat.

Meanwhile, carefully peel the pears, leaving the stalks intact. Add the pears to the pan and poach over a medium heat, covered with the lid, for 20–30 minutes or until tender, shaking the pan occasionally. The poaching liquid should be nice and syrupy; if not, remove the pears and reduce the spiced coffee over a high heat.

Meanwhile, make the coconut crumb. Place the flour, butter, sugar and coconut into a bowl and rub together with your fingers to the texture of breadcrumbs. Spread over the lined baking tray and bake for 10–15 minutes, or until golden. Set aside to cool.

Remove the pears from the heat and allow to cool slightly in the spiced coffee mixture. Transfer to a bowl and chill (or serve warm, if preferred).

To serve, place a pear in a shallow serving dish, strain the coffee syrup over the top and scatter over some of the coconut crumb.

SUNSHINE BANANA BREAD
WITH HONEYED MASCARPONE

Banana bread is extremely popular in the Caribbean and everyone has their own favourite recipe. This is one of mine – it's an easy recipe and I love the addition of coconut and walnuts, which add a lovely texture. Banana bread is great at any time of the day: for a mid-afternoon snack, as a dessert, or even for breakfast with your morning coffee or tea. Try toasting a slice before serving with my honeyed mascarpone – yum!

125g unsalted butter,
    plus extra for greasing
100g soft brown sugar
2 large eggs, beaten
2 ripe bananas, mashed
50g walnuts, chopped
1½ tsp vanilla extract
1 tbsp shredded coconut
1 tbsp milk
225g plain flour
1 tsp baking powder
½ tsp bicarbonate of soda
1 tsp mixed spice
extra drizzle of honey,
    to serve (optional)

**For the Honeyed
    Mascarpone**
250g tub of mascarpone
1 tbsp icing sugar
1 tbsp honey
zest and juice of ½ lemon

Preheat the oven to 200°C/180°C fan/gas 6. Butter and line a loaf tin with baking parchment.

In a large bowl, beat together the butter and sugar until thick and creamy. Add the eggs, bananas, walnuts, vanilla extract, coconut and milk, and gently stir together until well combined. Sift in the flour, baking powder, bicarbonate of soda and mixed spice and gently fold in. Pour into the loaf tin and bake for 40–45 minutes, or until an inserted skewer comes out clean.

Leave the banana bread to cool in the tin for about 10 minutes and then turn out onto a wire rack to cool completely ... if you can wait that long!

Meanwhile, make the honeyed mascarpone. In a bowl, blend together the mascarpone, sugar, honey, lemon zest and juice, until well combined.

Serve slices of the banana bread topped with a spoonful of the honeyed mascarpone and drizzled with a little more honey, if you like.

DRINKS

BITTER ORANGE & CARDAMOM MARTINI

I simply couldn't visit Ian Fleming's Jamaican villa without making a Martini in his honour. So, here is my Bitter Orange and Cardamom Martini; in true James Bond style, it's shaken and not stirred!

SERVES 4

8 cardamom pods
3 tbsp bitter orange
   marmalade
450ml vodka
3 orange peel strips
150ml Cointreau
   or triple sec
2 tbsp fresh lemon juice
3 large splashes
   Angostura bitters

For the garnish
4 x orange peel twists

In a pestle and mortar, crush the cardamom pods until they have split open.

In a small saucepan, melt the marmalade over a medium heat, but do not allow to boil. Remove from the heat and add the vodka, crushed cardamom pods and orange peel strips. Set aside to infuse until cool.

Pour the cooled mixture into a cocktail shaker filled with ice. Add the Cointreau, lemon juice and Angostura bitters and give everything a good shake.

Fine-strain into Martini glasses and serve garnished with orange peel twists.

TIP: To make the orange peel twists, using a paring knife or peeler, cut a long thin piece of peel from the orange (try to avoid digging into the pith). Roll the strip of peel into a spiral and give it a little squeeze to tighten the twist before dropping into your drink.

BLUEWATER BREEZE

The bluest sea rippled by a perfect breeze under the Tobagan sun
is the inspiration behind this banging cocktail! It's simple to make,
but beautifully delivers.

SERVES 2

a large handful of ice cubes
50ml vodka
50ml white rum
230ml coconut water
2 tbsp blue Curaçao
2 tbsp coconut cream
100ml pineapple juice,
   to top up
fresh pineapple slices,
   to serve

Fill a cocktail shaker with ice and add the vodka, rum, coconut
water, blue Curaçao and coconut cream. Put the lid on and get
shaking! Pour into two tall glasses, top up with the pineapple
juice and garnish with a slice of fresh fruit.

CARIBBEAN SORREL COCKTAIL

Sorrel is the Jamaican word for the hibiscus, a flower grown in many parts of the Caribbean. This slightly tart and tangy spiced drink is traditionally served at Christmas, but can be enjoyed at any time of the year. If you're using fresh sorrel/hibiscus, make sure that you remove the nut or seed as it can be quite bitter. The sorrel infusion can also be served with lemonade for a refreshing non-alcoholic beverage.

SERVES 2

For the sorrel infusion
2 litres water
500g dried red sorrel
    flower buds
3 cinnamon sticks
8 cloves
2 star anise
50g fresh root ginger, sliced
3 strips of orange peel
3–4 tbsp sugar, to taste

For the cocktail
ice cubes
200ml sorrel infusion
    (see above)
125ml white rum
juice of 1 lime
lime and orange slices,
    to garnish

To make the infusion, put all of the ingredients into a large saucepan set over a medium-high heat and bring to the boil. Reduce the heat and simmer for 8–10 minutes. Remove from the heat and cover with a lid to allow the flower buds and aromatics to steep and cool. This is best left for 6–8 hours in the fridge.

Pass the cooled infusion through a fine sieve.

To make the cocktail, fill a cocktail shaker with ice cubes and add the sorrel infusion, rum and lime juice. Shake well, then pour into two glasses over fresh ice and garnish with lime and orange slices.

CARIBBEAN COCONUT CHAI

Chai is a spiced milk tea from India and this is my Trinidadian twist
with the flavours of coconut and tonka bean. If you can't find tonka bean,
you can use a couple of cloves and a pinch of nutmeg or half a vanilla
pod in the infusion.

SERVES 4

400ml boiling water
2–3 tbsp loose black
  tea leaves
seeds from 10 crushed
  green cardamom pods
  (pods discarded)
1 cinnamon stick, broken
6 slices of fresh root ginger
1 x 400ml tin coconut milk
1 tonka bean, for grating
1 tbsp caster sugar,
  or to taste
nutmeg, for grating
  (optional)

Combine the boiling water and tea leaves in a saucepan and
infuse the tea to your preferred strength. Strain to remove the tea
leaves and return the tea infusion to the pan. Add the cardamom
seeds, cinnamon, ginger and coconut milk and give everything
a good stir. Grate in half of the tonka bean and set the pan over a
low-medium heat. Bring to a gentle simmer and cook for 5 minutes
to allow the flavours to infuse, but do not boil. Add sugar to taste,
stir until dissolved and remove from the heat.

To serve, strain or ladle into glasses or cups and garnish with
a grating of tonka bean or nutmeg.

CORN 'N' OIL

Velvet Falernum, with its strange-sounding name, is a bartender's
dream – it's a spicy, sweet syrup that adds a sweet kick to many tropical
cocktails. The 'oil' in this golden corn-coloured cocktail comes from the
black strap rum, which, before stirring, sits on top of the drink, like...
well, a puddle of oil. Trust me, though, it's delicious!

SERVES 1

large ice cubes
60ml black strap rum
   or dark rum
15ml Velvet Falernum
15ml fresh lime juice
2–3 dashes Angostura
   bitters
lime slices, to garnish

Fill a rocks glass with ice and pour in the rum, falernum,
lime juice and bitters. Give everything a quick stir and
garnish with a fresh lime slices.

DEATH BY CHOCOLATE MARTINI

Martinis are nearly always gin-or vodka-based, but this is not a clean-cut Martini as we know it. Instead, I give you a delectable, creamy chocolate and vodka sensation in a glass, which ends with the sweet smell and taste of cardamom on one's lips. Death by chocolate, indeed.

SERVES 2

1 tbsp cocoa powder
½ tsp ground cardamom
175ml chocolate liqueur,
    plus extra for decorating
100ml vodka
75ml single cream
ice cubes

First, decorate the glasses. Mix together the cocoa powder and ground cardamom on one plate, then pour a few tablespoons of chocolate liqueur into a separate small saucer. Carefully and gently dip the rim of each Martini glass into the liqueur, making sure the entire rim is coated, then dip into the cocoa and cardamom mixture, to coat. Set aside.

Add the chocolate liqueur, vodka and single cream to a cocktail shaker filled with ice and shake for 20 seconds. Carefully pour into the decorated glasses and enjoy!

COCONUT, PINEAPPLE & MANGO MINT COOLER

This cooler is so fresh and vibrant it doesn't need any alcohol.
It's the sweet tropical taste of the Caribbean in a glass!

SERVES 4

1 small pineapple,
    peeled and diced
2 large mangos,
    peeled and diced
2 x 400ml tins
    coconut milk
a handful of mint,
    roughly chopped
1 tsp caster sugar,
    plus extra to taste
a handful of ice cubes,
    plus extra to serve

To garnish
pineapple wedges
mint sprigs

Put the pineapple and mango into a sturdy blender and pour over the coconut milk. Add the chopped mint, 1 teaspoon of sugar and a large handful of ice. Blend until smooth and taste for sweetness, adding a little more sugar if required. If the mixture is too thick, add a dash of water and pulse again.

Pour into glasses filled with a little ice and garnish with pineapple wedges and sprigs of mint.

RUM

Of course, I can't talk about the Caribbean without saying a few words about rum. The Caribbean is a huge producer of both white and dark rum.

Rum is said to have been first distilled in Barbados in the seventeenth century. As Europeans began colonising the islands, the sugar-cane plantations became an important part of the trade industry and African slaves were made to work on the fields. Sugar was the main product of the crops, but sugar cane molasses (the by-product of refining sugar) was used to create alcohol. The vast majority of rum is produced from molasses, which provides the rich, dark flavours associated with the spirit, but it can also be made from pressed sugarcane juice, resulting in a lighter, grassier-tasting rum (rhum agricole). In the early days, rum was distilled in pot stills, before modern, sophisticated column stills allowed for easier mass production. Premium rums are stored and aged in oak barrels, which mellow its natural harshness .

The drink is an important part of Caribbean culture and rum shops are a great place to meet and chat with the locals. They're not really bars or shops – they can be in people's houses or in shacks on the beach or roadside and you can buy bottles of rum to drink as you enjoy the vibe. There are plenty of rums to choose from and they all have a distinct flavour – rum tasting is one of the many joys of a trip to the Caribbean!

Just as the different islands have their own food specialities, they also have their own flavours of rum. Jamaican rum, for instance, is thick and sweet with fermented notes, whereas Saint Lucian rum is rich and robust. The Angostura Gran Anejo is a seven-year-old rum from Angostura in Trinidad (well known for its Angostura Bitters), which features aromas of dried fruit with vanilla and wonderful Christmas spices. Another popular spiced rum, Chairman's Reserve Spiced Rum, is made in Saint Lucia and contains flavours of clove and allspice. If you're looking for a more traditional rum, there is the Mount Gay Eclipse Gold from Barbados, or the famous English Harbour 1981 from Antigua (which some say is the best in the Caribbean). For a special occasion, one of my favourites is from Trinidad: Plantation Single Cask Rum, an aged rum matured in bourbon casks... superb! Coconut rum is also popular throughout the Caribbean and is great in cocktails.

Rum is used in many regional dishes. One of my favourites is a butter rum cake I tried in Antigua and I've included the recipe on page 187 for you to try. The tipple forms the base of many tropical cocktails – my mum's Rum Punch (page 235) is definitely a winner!

MANGO & COCONUT RUM DAIQUIRI

Mangos are a celebrated fruit in the Caribbean – there are annual mango festivals on many of the islands – and they are a main ingredient in lots of traditional dishes, sweet or savoury. The fruits are juicy, sweet and larger than any mangos we get over here. I made this sumptuous mango cocktail on the beach in Saint Lucia after sundown – a perfect end to the day. You can either make the purée by blending fresh mangos in a blender until smooth or you can buy it ready-prepared.

SERVES 2

200ml mango purée
juice of 1 lime
1–2 tbsp sugar syrup
    (depending on how
    sweet you like it!)
150ml coconut rum
a large handful of ice

fresh mango slices,
    to garnish
mint sprigs, to garnish

Combine the mango purée, lime juice, sugar syrup, coconut rum and ice in a blender and blitz until smooth.

Pour into tall glasses and garnish each with a mango slice and a sprig of fresh mint.

RUM PU PUNCH

For the last day of filming I just had to make up some of my Mum's delicious rum punch – it's a family favourite and I love it... and so did the crew! You can leave out the rum if you prefer a non-alcoholic punch, but remember – more rum, more dancing!

SERVES 14–16

175ml boiling water
175g granulated sugar
juice of 4 limes and 4 lemons
1 tsp Angostura bitters
400ml mango purée
150ml strawberry purée
300ml white rum
1 litre tropical fruit juice
1 litre lemonade
plenty of ice cubes, to serve
lime wedges and orange
    slices, to garnish
freshly grated nutmeg,
    to garnish

In a medium saucepan set over a medium heat, stir together the sugar and water until dissolved, then set aside until cold.

In a large pitcher, mix the cold sugar syrup with the lime and lemon juice, Angostura bitters, mango and strawberry purées and the rum. Stir together until well mixed and chill.

When ready to serve, stir in the fruit juice and lemonade. Serve over ice, garnished with lime and orange slices and a sprinkling of freshly grated nutmeg.

TROPICAL FIZZY PERFECTION!

This fizzy cocktail is an elegant, tropical delight and is perfect for a special occasion or summer barbecue. Cheers!

SERVES 4–6

150g fresh raspberries
100g tinned lychees
    (drained weight)
1 mango, peeled
    and diced
2–3 tbsp lime syrup
Champagne, to top up

Put the raspberries, lychees, mango and lime syrup into a food processor or blender and purée until smooth. Pass through a fine sieve into a bowl and set aside.

To serve, spoon 1½ tablespoons of the fruit purée into chilled Champagne flutes, then top up with Champagne. Give everything a quick swizzle, kick back, sip and savour!

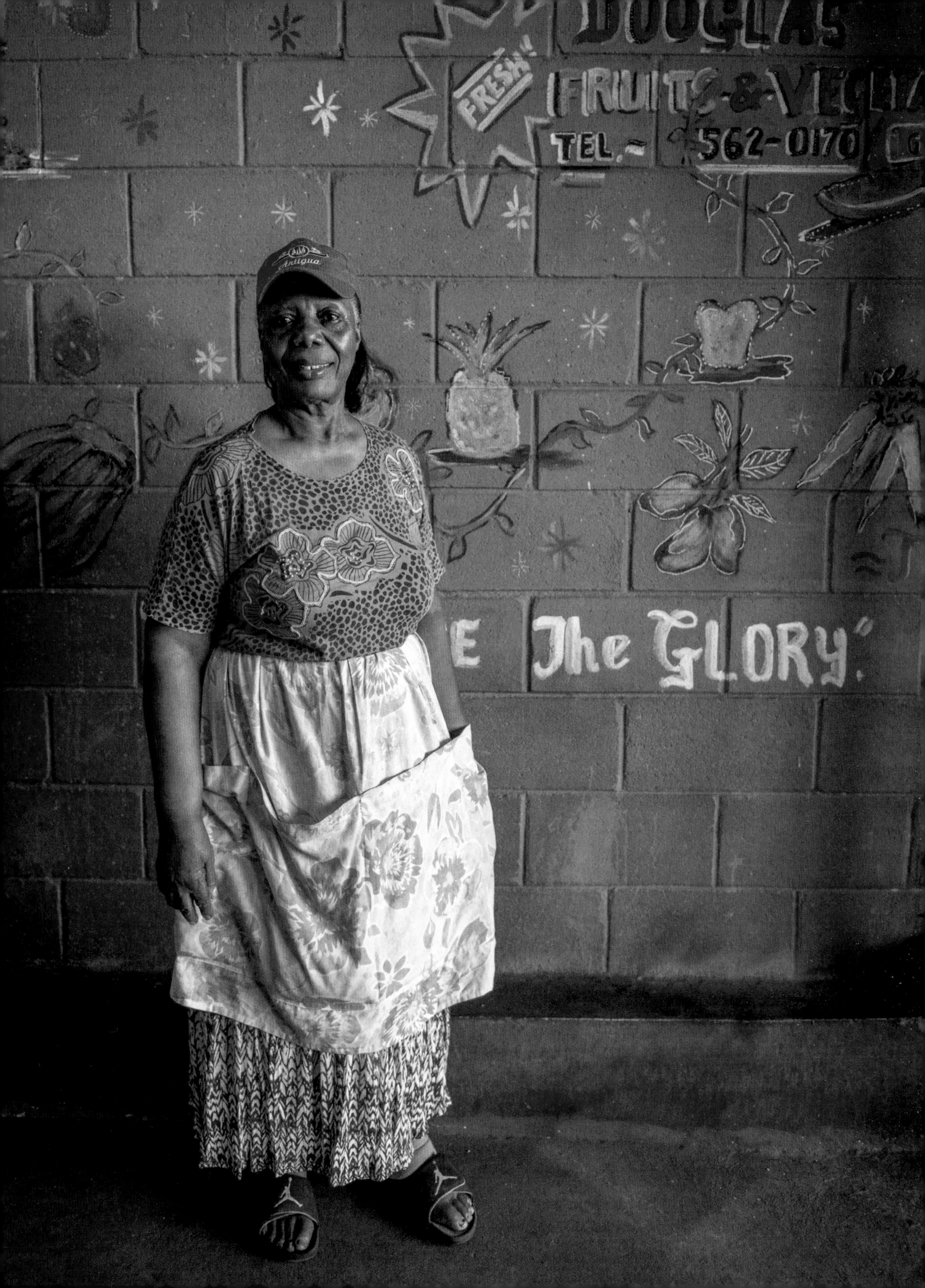
FRESH!
TEL.
562-0170
Antigua
The GLORY".

INGREDIENTS

ACKEE
Closely related to the lychee, ackee is a fruit that is slightly sour in flavour and starchy in texture. It's the national fruit of Jamaica and part of the traditional dish of Ackee and Saltfish (see page 14). It can be bought tinned from some supermarkets and Afro-Caribbean grocers.

AVOCADO
Avocados grow large in the Caribbean climate, where they are referred to as 'pear'. They are deliciously creamy too.

BEANS AND PEAS
Many types of beans and peas are used throughout the Caribbean as a convenient protein source, including black beans, gungo peas, black-eyed peas and yellow and green split peas. Red kidney beans are also commonly used, but confusingly they are called 'peas' when cooked in Rice 'n' Peas (see page 136).

CALLALOO
A leafy vegetable popular across the Caribbean islands, callaloo is eaten like spinach. It can be bought fresh from Afro-Caribbean grocers or tinned in some supermarkets. Get the fresh stuff if you can or substitute callaloo with spinach or kale.

COCONUT
Mostly availble in the UK are the older, dark brown coconuts. In the Caribbean coconuts are also enjoyed when they are young and green, not just for the refreshing coconut water inside but also the delicious jellied flesh.

COCONUT MILK
Coconut milk can be made by grating coconut flesh into hot water and leaving it to soak before squeezing through a fine cloth to extract the white liquid. Fortunately, it is also sold in handy tins which saves time. Coconut milk is an important ingredient in soups, curries and rundown.

FRUIT
The Caribbean islands enjoy an abundance of tropical fruits, from the familiar yellow and green bananas, pineapple, mangoes and passionfruit to the lesser known pawpaw (papaya), guava, soursop and sweetsop. While they are incredible when eaten fresh and ripe, they are even better in my Warm Tropical Fruits in Spiced Rum with (see page 182).

GINGER
Of all the Caribbean islands, Jamaica is most closely associated with ginger. It is used in sweet and savoury dishes, as well as beer.

GOAT
A popular meat in Caribbean cooking, most often eaten in slow-cooked curries. Mutton or lamb can be used as a substitute.

GROUND PROVISIONS/ ISLAND PROVISIONS/ HARD FOODS
Hearty, starchy foods, such as green bananas, yam, dasheen and boiled dumplings, are eaten alongside other dishes. Most commonly used in soups and also boiled to be eaten as 'hard food'.

JERK SEASONING
A blend of spices, vegetables and herbs, including pimento seeds, scotch bonnet peppers, spring onions and fresh thyme that is an intergral part of jerk dishes. Recipes can vary and are often kept secret, but most contain a base of these ingredients.

LIME
The citrus zing of lime brings a freshness to any dish. Both lime juice and zest is used more

frequently in Caribbean dishes than lemon.

LOTUS ROOT
Fresh lotus root is available from Asian supermarkets and although it's sometimes difficult to find, it's worth it. Tinned lotus root just isn't quite the same.

MACKEREL
Tinned mackerel is a staple ingredient in Caribbean kitchens, which is used in dishes such as mackerel rundown. Fresh mackerel is equally popular. I use fresh fillets in the traditional recipe for Mackerel Escovitch (see page 119).

NUTMEG
Nutmeg is an amazing aromatic spice. It can be bought ready ground, however, for freshness I prefer to grate a little whole nutmeg into dishes.

OKRA
A popular vegetable used in many vegetarian dishes, which can sometimes have a slightly slimy, sticky texture that works well to thicken stews and soups. Okra has quite a mild flavour so it works well in spicy dishes.

OXTAIL
The tail of cattle that is braised slowly in a popular Caribbean dish. Oxtail benefits from hours of slow cooking to become tender and rich. Try Peppy's Braised Oxtail with Butterbeans (see page 164).

PIMENTO
One of the most popular spices in the Caribbean, pimento is sold both as whole dried berries and a ground powder. It's more commonly known as 'allspice' in the UK. The berries add an incredible aroma to stews.

PLANTAIN
Although related to the banana, plantain is never eaten raw. It is commonly fried or boiled, or can even be made into fries.

RICE
A mainstay of Caribbean food, especially as part of the classic dish Rice 'n' Peas (see page 136). Long-grain or basmati rice are most often used.

SNAPPER
This firm-fleshed fish is one of the Caribbean's most popular. Plus it tastes great, especially in my Mustard Snapper with Mango Chilli Chow (see page 122). If you can't find snapper, use bass or bream in its place.

SWEET POTATO
Added to soups and curries, sweet potatoes are more commonly used than potatoes. Flesh colours vary from cream, yellow, orange and even purple.

SALTFISH
This preserved fish is best know as part of Jamaica's national dish, Ackee and Saltfish. Before cooking, it needs to be soaked in water and boiled to remove any excess salt.

SCOTCH BONNET
The distinctive hot chilli pepper used in many Caribbean dishes. To make the chilli less spicy, de-seed the scotch bonnet before cooking. Always wash your hands after handling them.

SPRING ONIONS
With a milder taste than ordinary onions, spring onions are used throughout the Caribbean, where they are known as 'scallions'.

TURMERIC
This bright yellow spice lends a strong flavour to curries and patties.

THYME
A key ingredient in jerk seasoning, this aromatic herb gives a unique flavour to many dishes. It is used both fresh and dried.

YAMS
Yams come in a variety of shapes, sizes and flesh colours, with the most common shades being yellow and white. Peeled and then either steamed or boiled to make a filling carbohydrate that is part of 'hard foods'.

ACKNOWLEDGEMENTS

What a pleasure it has been to create this book with such a lovely
and professional group of people.

Thank you to the entire team at Blue Marlin for helping to make a dream
come true with my Caribbean Kitchen. There are so many of you to thank.
What a crew! We enjoyed a wonderful journey together.

Thank you to all at Random House for rekindling my love for cookery
writing, especially as it was focused on the food and culture that is so close
to my heart. A big thank you to my publisher Lizzy and my editor Lisa. And
not forgetting photographer Dan, food stylist Bianca, prop stylist Tamzin
and designers Alex & Emma – guys, I want to eat every page!

To my family at JHA who are always there for me – Jerry, Sarah, Julie
and the inspirational Charlotte.

To my close family and friends, my loved ones, my kids and my
adorable dog Bobby – thank you!

INDEX

Haiti

Dominican
Republic

Jamaica

CARIBBEAN SEA